The Precepts and Doctrines of Men

Duane Radcliffe and Marcus Ross

iUniverse, Inc.
New York   Bloomington

The Precepts and Doctrines of Men

iUniverse books may be ordered through booksellers or by contacting:

iUniverse
1663 Liberty Drive
Bloomington, IN 47403
www.iuniverse.com
1-800-Authors (1-800-288-4677)

ISBN: 978-1-4502-5116-7 (sc)
ISBN: 978-1-4502-5117-4 (ebk)

Printed in the United States of America

iUniverse rev. date: 08/10/2010

In The Precepts and Doctrines of Men, by authors Duane Radcliffe and Marcus Ross, readers are given a resounding echo of biblical injunctions that blast away human encumbrances from the Word of God.

The authors have examined biblical texts in remarkable detail, tracing crucial words to their linguistic source. Laying aside the traditions of man, they present coherent interpretations of biblical events and themes. What was the reality of the Tree of Knowledge of Good and Evil in the Garden of Eden? The deity of Christ and the nature of the Church are considered. It also explains in detail whether the rapture is true or not, and at last brings clear understanding of the parable of the fig tree.

This book is vital in recognizing the traditions of men that obscure the Word of God. "You have captured the teachings that are wanted and sought after by many millions of people."
—Mark Maine

Over a period of eight years, authors DUANE RADCLIFFE and MARCUS ROSS have studied the Word of God in exhaustive detail, using scholarly works both in print and software

Isa. 29:13

13. Wherefore the Lord said, Forasmuch as this people draw near me with their mouth, and with their lips do honour me, but have removed their heart far from me, and their fear toward tile is taught by the precept of men: (KJV)

Mark 7:13

13. Making the word of God of none effect through your tradition, which ye have delivered: and many such like things do ye. (KJV)

Contents

Authors' Note

We acknowledge that all text of scripture used in this book comes from the King James Version of the Bible (KJV). When we extracted the meanings of these words, they are from Strong's Exhaustive Concordance. The numbers before each meaning denote Strong's numbers and can be looked up in Strong's Concordance. In the case of different meanings, it is noted that there are, in most cases, different meanings for each word.

The authors therefore underlined for clarity the meanings that applied to the context of the point being made in that particular instance. Also we underlined portions of the Scripture being used to help the reader to understand fully what were the main points of the Scripture being quoted. Special thanks goes to Bible Soft, which created the PC Study Bible. This has been an extremely valuable asset in looking up the meanings, and also being able to go into the manuscripts and look at the original way the Bible was written.

Introduction

Through years of studying God's Word, the authors have realized that there is a lot in Scripture that is not being taught in the churches today. We also learned that there is a lot of misunderstanding of certain aspects of the Word that through man's precepts and traditions, we found a lot of incorrect information is being presented to readers who are trying to find the truth in biblical teachings. We are going to endeavor to present in this book, subjects on which we feel we can prove by Scripture some truths that we feel the Holy Spirit revealed to us. We will cover some controversial subjects that we feel have not been explored before.

- The Serpent in the Garden of Eden was not what most people are taught as a snake coiled around a tree with a forked tongue sticking out. This was a symbol of a true living being.

- The fruit that was eaten in the garden was not an apple or a pomegranate or any other such fruit. This was a figure of speech to signify knowledge that they acquired.

- Were there other humans created before Adam was formed, to explain why there are different nationalities in this world today?

- Was it God's plan that Adam and Eve should fall in order for God to implement his plan of Salvation through the Messiah?

- Was racism created by the Serpent (Satan) in the Garden of Eden? Is it God's desire for people to separate themselves from others of their species in order to show that they are superior to others?

- Are there seeds of the Serpent as spoken of in Genesis 3:15, which are still in this world, and are today getting a one- world system ready for the coming of Antichrist?

- Did these sons of Satan have a name that can be documented in Scripture, and did Jesus himself identify who they were? History also will reflect how the sons of the Serpent (Satan) have behaved throughout history. Have they plundered mankind in the name of God, made him a slave not only literally but also figuratively with a system of controlling the governments of this world, keeping the citizens of this world as a whole in bondage and slavery?

- Is the tradition in some churches of speaking in tongues a truism according to Scripture, or is it a tradition that was spawned to confuse and distract most Christians from the truth? There are other traditions concerning the Communion, which are not scriptural.

- What about the seven churches in Revelation chapters 2 and 3? Were these the churches of Paul and John's day, or are they end- time churches during the great tribulation? Can we learn from Scripture about the two witnesses? Will the Church or Body of Christ be here during the great tribulation or will its members be raptured from this earth?

It is the authors' fervent hope that as you read this book you will come away with a new light on these subjects. The authors do not want to imply that the biblical teachings are not proper. We support spiritual teachings. It is not just in the Bible that things are different than what they seem but in all facets of life. We need to use the power of thought as was given to us by our creator to not make rash judgements, but check things out for our self. This not only includes the church but the media, Politics, gossip and other thought processes to which we come upon everyday in our lives. Think for yourselves and not be influenced by others. "You may not agree with what is written in this book, but if you search for yourselves the meanings of the scriptures for you own understanding, then this book is a success." Your thought process and intuition will guide you along with meditation, getting guidance from the Infinite mind of the universe which created all things. The Bible is filled with euphemism and figures of speech along with parables so that the reader needs to not just gloss over some passage but check it out throughly to be sure the meaning is understood.

The main theme of this book is quoted from the book of Ephesians.

Eph. 6:12
- For we wrestle not against flesh and blood, but against principalities, against powers, against the rulers of the darkness of this world, against spiritual wickedness in high places. (KJV)

Here Paul describes the real fight in this world. Things are usually not as they seem as you will find out as you read through this book. It is not only a physical battle but a spiritual one as well.

Read with prayer and meditation and you may see a whole new meaning on life and the world as we know it. Now let's begin chapter 1.

1

Who Was the Serpent in the Garden of Eden?

The Serpent

Many doctrines have depicted a snake in a tree tempting Eve. Pictures have been painted showing a snake coiled around a tree. Is this the true image of what really happened or is there a different perspective on it? Let us go into what the Bible account says in Genesis 3:1- 5.

1. Now the <u>serpent</u> was more <u>subtle</u> than any <u>beast</u> of the field which the Lord God has made. And <u>he said unto the woman,</u> "Yea, hath God said, ye shall not eat of every tree of the garden?"

2. And the woman said unto the serpent, We may eat of the fruit of the trees of the garden:

3. But of the fruit of the tree which is in the midst of the garden, God hath said, ye shall not eat of it, neither shall ye touch it, lest ye die.

4. And the serpent said unto the woman, Ye shall not surely die:

5. For God doth know that in the day ye eat thereof, then your eyes shall be opened, and <u>ye shall be as gods,</u> knowing good and evil. (KJV)

What we see in these passages is that the Serpent talked to Eve. Now I do not know of any serpents that talk to this day. In fact the only animal in the Bible that talked was Baalam's Ass. So this must have been a special kind of serpent. According to *Strongs' Exhaustive Concordance,* we see that the word **serpent** means the following.

5175 nachash (naw-khawsh');
from 5172; a snake <u>(from its hiss):</u>

To get a clearer picture of the meaning of this word and to note that it has a hiss, we will now go to the root word of the meaning 5172.

5172 nachash (naw-khash');
A primitive root; properly, to <u>hiss, i.e., whisper a (magic) spell;</u> generally, to <u>prognosticate:</u>

When we go to the word **whisper,** we find the *American Heritage Dictionary* has the following meanings:

A <u>secretly or surreptitiously expressed belief, rumor, or hint:</u> *whispers of scandal*
To say or <u>tell privately or secretly</u>
To speak quietly and privately, as by way of <u>gossip, slander,</u> or intrigue.'

The word **whisper** will be of interest to the readers, when we get into chapter 5, The High Cabal and the New World Order.

Prognosticate has a relative meaning, when we look into the *American Heritage Dictionary* and see what the meaning of this word is.

Prog-nos-ti-cate

1. To <u>predict according to present indications</u> or <u>signs; foretell.</u> See Synonyms at PREDICT.

2. To foreshadow; portend: urban architectural that prognosticates a social and cultural renaissance.

[Middle English pronosticaten, from Medieval Latin prognosticare, prognosticat-, from Latin prognosticum, sign of the future, from Greek prognostikon, from neuter of prognostikos. Foreknowing. See Prognostic].

Prognosticate then means to predict events. This is what the Serpent did when he told Eve, that "you can be as gods." Now in verse 1 we also read that the Serpent was more subtle than any beasts. The word *subtle,* in Hebrew, has the following meaning:

6175 'aruwm (aw-room');
passive participle of 6191; cunning (usually in a bad sense):

Breaking this word down, we get a clearer idea of what is said:

6191 'aram (aw-ram');
a primitive root; properly, to be (or make) bare; but used only in the derivative sense (through the idea perhaps of smoothness) to be cunning (usually in a bad sense):

Looking at these meanings, we see the Serpent's true character. He is cunning in a bad sense, he is smooth. Does this remind you of someone all Christians should know about? He is also referred to as a beast in this first verse. Looking into the Hebrew meaning of *beast,* we find a different meaning than this word implies.

2416 chay (khah'-ee);
from 2421; <u>alive;</u> hence, <u>raw (flesh);</u> fresh (plant, water, year), strong; also (as noun, especially in the feminine singular and masculine plural) life (or <u>living thing),</u> whether literally or figuratively:

After a closer look at the word *beast,* we see that it does not necessarily mean an animal but has the meaning of something alive, or a living thing. The word *chay* is also used in Genesis 2:7 for the word *living.*

7.   And the Lord God formed man of the dust of the ground, and breathed into his nostrils the breath of life; and man became a *living* soul. (KJV)

There is a word for the literal meaning of *beast* found in Jeremiah.

Jer 12:4

4.   How long shall the land mourn, and the herbs of every field wither, for the wickedness of them that dwell therein? the <u>beasts</u> are consumed, and the birds; because they said, He shall not see our last end.(KJV)

According to *Strong's Concordance,* that word *beast* means the following:

929 behemah (be-hay-maw');
from an unused root (probably <u>meaning to be mute);</u> properly, a <u>dumb beast;</u> especially any large <u>quadruped or animal</u> (often collective):

With these meanings understood, it should

become clear that this was not a snake, as we know it. Somehow it has been added into Christian teaching, that Satan got into a snake and spake to Eve, even though there is no Scripture that supports this theory. The word *Serpent,* is linked to Satan himself throughout Scripture. In other words the Serpent is the Devil. Written proof is found in Revelation.

Rev. 12:7-9.

7. And there was war in heaven: Michael and his angels fought against the dragon; and the dragon fought and his angels,

8. And prevailed not; neither was their place found any more in heaven.

9. And the great dragon was cast out, that <u>old serpent, called the Devil,</u> and <u>Satan,</u> which deceiveth the whole world: he was cast out into the earth, and his angels were cast out with him. (KJV)

This prediction is an end- time prophecy and will be explained in another chapter. Also in Revelation 20:1- 2, we read the following:

Rev. 20:1-2

1. And I saw an angel come down from heaven, having the key of the bottomless pit and a great chain in his hand.

2. And he laid hold on the dragon, that <u>old serpent,</u> which is the <u>Devil,</u> and <u>Satan,</u> and bound him a thousand years, (KJV)

In the authors' experience, through our study of Scripture that the word *Serpent* is used throughout Scripture referring to Satan in most cases. Even the words crook or crooked Serpent, still means Satan. The prophet Isaiah gives this account of the Serpent:

Isa. 27:1

1. In that day the Lord with his sore and great and strong sword shall punish leviathan the piercing serpent, even <u>leviathan</u> that crooked <u>serpent;</u> and he shall slay the dragon that is in the sea. (KJV)

The word *leviathan* has the following meaning in the Hebrew:

3882 livyathan (liv-yaw-thawn');
from 3867; a wreathed animal, i.e., <u>a serpent</u> (especially the crocodile or some other large sea monster); figuratively, <u>the constellation of the dragon;</u> also as a symbol of Bab.:

This shows that Satan is called by many names, even using Leviathan to show that God was talking about Satan in this verse. It was interesting to the authors when we looked up the meaning of the word *constellation.*

1. *Astronomy.* a. <u>An arbitrary formation of stars</u> perceived as a figure or design, especially one of 88 recognized groups named after characters from classical mythology and various common animals and objects. b. An area of the celestial sphere occupied by one of the 88 recognized constellations.

4. A <u>set of configuration, as of related items, properties, ideas, or individuals:</u> a constellation of demands ranging from better food to improved health care; a constellation of feelings about the divorce.

In reference to definition 1, we find written in Revelation about the world that was, or before this earth age of Satan and how the constellation image is used referring to Satan and his activities.

Rev. 12:1-4

1. And there appeared a great <u>wonder in heaven;</u> a woman clothed with the sun, and the moon under her feet, and upon her head a crown of twelve stars:

2. And she is with child cried, travailing in birth, and pained to be delivered.

3. And there appeared another wonder in heaven; and behold a great red <u>dragon,</u> having seven heads and ten horns, and seven crowns upon his heads.

4. And his tail <u>drew the third part of the stars of heaven,</u> and did cast them to the earth: and <u>the dragon</u> stood before the woman which was ready to be delivered, for to devour her child as it was born. (KJV)

Job also describes the **Serpent**, in this way.

Job 26:13

13. By his spirit he hath garnished the heavens; his hand hath formed the <u>crooked serpent.</u> (KJV)

As we look at the phrase "<u>The</u> Serpent," we will find that in the Hebrew and Greek and Chaldean: "The" is the definite article. Example, "Thus said the Lord." The article as the actual person, place or thing. So the Serpent is <u>the</u> Devil.

The Tree

Now we know, that the Serpent was the Devil in the garden. What is the tree of the knowledge of good and evil? The authors are not aware of any tree or fruit that will give us knowledge of good or evil or any knowledge of any kind. In a closer look at Genesis 3:2-3, we read:

Gen. 3:2-3

2.   And the woman said unto the serpent, We may eat of the <u>fruit</u> of the trees of the garden:

3.   But of the fruit of the <u>tree</u> which is in the midst of the garden, God hath said, ye shall not eat of it, neither <u>shall ye touch</u> it, lest ye die. (KJV)

Now as we look closely at the word *tree,* we undertake a very interesting study of the root meanings of this word, and there is a lot of hidden truth here. The word **tree** breaks down as follows.

6086 'ets (ates);
<u>from 6095;</u> a tree <u>(from its firmness);</u> hence, wood (plural sticks):

This sounds like a tree, until you break this word down to its prime root meaning.

6095 'atsah (aw-tsaw');
a primitive root; properly, <u>to fasten (or make firm), i.e., to close</u> (the eyes):

So therefore if something or someone has closed eyes, then this could not be a tree. The word *atsah* also can be broken down to *atseh,* which is a cognate of the same word.

6096 'atseh (aw-tseh');
from 6095; the <u>spine (as giving firmness to the body)</u>:

<u>It is interesting that the word originally should have been a spine or body, but the translators chose to give you the impression that this was only a tree. We will go into the reason why these techniques were used in chapters 3 and 4. Now as we link up the words to fasten,</u> or <u>make firm,</u> these meanings are referring to the spine. Then looking at all the definitions of tree, we see it indicates that there was a body with a spine, showing that it was a living and breathing being as indicated in Genesis 3:1: "as he was more subtle than any beast."

Knowing that the word *beast* means a living being, and tree breaks down to a body, then the Serpent was the tree of the knowledge of good and evil. Tree is used in other passages of Scripture as being a synonym for man. In Psalm chapter 1, we find this.

Ps. 1:1-3

1. Blessed is the <u>man</u> that walketh not in the counsel of the ungodly, nor standeth in the way of sinners, not sitteth in the seat of the scornful.

2. But his delight is in the law of the Lord; and in his law doth he meditate day and night.

3. And he shall be like a <u>tree</u> planted by the rivers of water, that bringeth forth his

fruit in his season; his <u>leaf</u> also shall not wither; and whatsoever he doeth shall prosper. (KJV)

Here then we see that man is likened unto a tree that brings forth fruit and we also see where leaf is used, which can refer to the fig leaves that Adam and Eve covered themselves with. Now Satan when he was created was the crowning cherub. For in Ezekiel we get the following account.

Ezek. 28:2-3

2. Son of man, say unto <u>the prince of Tyrus,</u> Thus saith the Lord GOD; Because thine heart is lifted up, and thou hast said, <u>I am a God,</u> I sit in the seat of God, in the midst of the seas; yet thou art <u>a man,</u> and not God, though thou set thine heart as the heart of God:

3. Behold, <u>thou art wiser than Daniel;</u> there is no secret that they can hide from thee: (KJV)

The first verse of this chapter alludes to the subject of this chapter as being the prince of Tyrus. If this be true, then how could he be wiser than Daniel, who was visited by Michael and Gabriel, who taught Daniel the secrets of God. To further demonstrate who is really the subject of this chapter, we will continue in Ezekiel.

Ezek. 28:13-22

13. <u>Thou hast been in Eden the garden of God;</u> every precious stone was thy covering, the sardius, topaz, and the diamond, the beryl, the onyx, and the jasper, the sapphire, the emerald, and the carbuncle, and gold: the

workmanship of thy tabrets and of thy pipes was prepared in thee in the day that thou wast created.

14. Thou art the <u>anointed cherub</u> that cover- eth; and I have set thee so: thou wast upon the holy mountain of God; thou hast walked up and down in the midst of the stones of fire.

15. Thou wast perfect in thy ways from the day that thou wast created, till iniquity was found in thee.

16. By the multitude of thy merchandise they have filled the midst of thee with violence, and thou hast sinned: therefore I will cast thee as profane out of the mountain of God: and I will destroy thee, 0 covering cherb, from the midst of the stones of fire. (KJV)

In verse 15 we read "Thou wast perfect in thy ways the day thou was created." So Satan knew good. He was the first creation of God and was created as perfect. We also see that iniquity was found in his heart, so he also had the knowledge of evil. Thus Satan was the tree of the knowledge of good and evil, as he was the only one who could have given this knowledge of good and evil. God is not a partaker of any evil, nor is evil in him, so he could not show Adam or Eve any evil. For proof that God does not participate in evil, is found in 1 John.

1 John 1:5

5. This then is the message which we have heard of him, and declare unto you, <u>that</u>

<u>God is light, and in him is no darkness at all</u>. (KJV)

The only entity that could possibly corrupt Adam and Eve was Satan, as he was in the Garden of Eden, as shown in Ezekiel 28:13.

To further document that the Serpent (Satan) was the tree in the Garden of Eden, we will go to Ezekiel and see where Satan is likened unto a tree.

Ezek. 31:2-18

2. Son of man, speak unto Pharaoh King of Egypt, and to his multitude; <u>Whom</u> art thou like in thy greatness?

3. Behold, the <u>Assyrian</u> was a cedar in Lebanon with fair branches, and with a shadowing shroud, and of a high stature; and his top was among the thick boughs.

4. The waters made him <u>great,</u> the deep set him up on high with her rivers running round about his plants, and sent out her little rivers unto all the <u>trees of the field.</u>

5. Therefore his height <u>was exalted above all the trees of the field,</u> and his <u>boughs were multiplied,</u> and his branches became long because of the multitude of waters, when he shot forth.

6. All the fowls of heaven made their nests in his boughs, and under his branches did all the beasts of the field bring forth their young, <u>and under his shadow dwelt all great nations.</u>

7. Thus was he fair in his greatness, in the

length of his branches: for his root was by great waters.

8. The <u>cedars in the garden of God</u> could not hide him: the fir <u>trees</u> were not like his boughs, and the <u>chestnut trees were</u> not like his branches; <u>nor any tree in the garden of God was like unto him in his beauty.</u>

9. <u>I have made him fair by the multitude of his branches: so that all the trees of Eden, that were in the garden of God, envied him.</u>

10. Therefore thus saith the Lord GOD; <u>because thou hast lifted up thyself</u> in <u>height, and he hath shot up his top among the thick boughs, and his heart is lifted up in his height.</u>

11. I have therefore delivered him into the hand of the mighty one of the heathen; he shall surely deal with him: <u>I have driven him out for his wickedness.</u>

12. And strangers, the terrible of the nations, have cut him off, and have left him: upon the mountains and in all the valleys his branches are fallen, and <u>his boughs are broken</u> by all the people of the earth are gone down from his shadow, and have left him. (KJV)

You can read the rest of this chapter for yourself, as we shortened it in this book because of the length and what seemed to be repetition. Going into the second verse, let's look at the meaning of <u>whom,</u> which has two meanings attached to it. The words used in the Hebrew are *El-Miy. El* means in this sense, upon, to, toward etc. *Miy* has the following meaning.

4310 miy (me);
an interrogative pronoun of persons, as 4100 is of things, who? Occasionally, <u>by a peculiar idiom, of things);</u> also (indefinitely) whoever; often used in oblique construction with prefix or suffix:

We see that God was using an **idiom.** Idiom has this meaning:

1. A speech form or an expression of a given language that is <u>peculiar to itself</u> grammatically or cannot be understood from the individual meanings of its elements, as in <u>keep tabs on</u>

God was saying unto Pharaoh that he was becoming similar to the Serpent (Satan) when he was in the Garden of Eden. In these verses trees are used to mean people, or a person. These verses of Ezekiel are talking about what happened before the overthrow of Lucifer, before he was called the Serpent or Satan. Documenting that Satan (Serpent) was called Lucifer in the world that then was, we go into Isaiah.

Isa. 14:12-15

5. How art thou fallen from heaven, <u>0 Lucifer,</u> son of the morning! how art thou cut down to the ground, which didst <u>weaken the nations!</u>

6. For thou hast said in thine heart, I will ascend into heaven, I <u>will exalt my throne above the stars of God:</u> I will <u>sit also upon</u>

the <u>mount of the congregation,</u> in the sides of the north:

7. I will <u>ascend above the heights of the clouds;</u> I will <u>be like the most High.</u>

8. Yet <u>thou shalt be brought down to hell, to the sides of the pit.</u> (KJV)

Going back into Ezekiel, it is interesting to note that several different kinds of trees are used in verse 8. We will go into the different people represented in a later chapter. Verse 18 is used to show that the Serpent (Satan) was in the Garden of Eden, along with others.

Ezek. 31:18

18. To whom art thou thus like in glory and in greatness among the <u>trees of Eden?</u> Yet shalt thou be brought <u>down with the trees of Eden unto the nether parts of the earth:</u> thou shalt lie in the midst of the uncircumcised with them that be slain by the sword. <u>This is Pharaoh</u> and all his multitude, saith the Lord GOD. (KJV)

When Satan is spoken of as the "Serpent," it is a figure of speech, i.e., an implied resemblance or representation. It does not literally mean a snake any more than it does when Dan is called a "Serpent" in Gen. 49:17; or when Herod is called a "fox" in Luke 13:32; or when Judah is call a "lion's whelp" Gen. 49:9. It is the same figure of speech when "doctrine" is called "leaven" in Matt. 16:6. These phrases are also called euphemisms, of which the *American Heritage Dictionary* defines as follows.

eu·phe·mism

The act or an example of substituting <u>a mild indirect, or vague term for one considered harsh, blunt, or offensive;</u> Euphemisms such as "slumber room" . . . abound in the funeral business" (Jessica Mitford).

1. The use of a word or phrase that is less expressive or direct but considered less distasteful, less offensive, etc. than another

2. A word or phrase so substituted; as <u>"she is at rest,"</u> is a euphemism for "she is dead."

The word *euphemism* will be important as we will use this in subsequent chapters. Following the point about a euphemism, we find that the Serpent in Genesis was condemned to eat dust as quoted in Genesis.

Gen. 3:14

14. And the Lord God said unto the serpent, Because thou hast done this, thou art cursed above all cattle, and above every beast of the field; upon thy belly shalt thou go, and <u>dust shall thou eat </u>all the days of thy life: (KJV)

This is a figure of speech or a metaphor, as we know that Satan or the Serpent does not literally eat dust, but if we look at this phrase, the word *dust* represents man, as man was formed from the dust of the earth. Therefore the figure of speech of the Serpent eating dust is not a truism, as snakes in reality do not eat dust. Then as man was created from dust, and when he dies his body turns to dust, this would be a modern metaphor that Satan would be responsible for all the lost souls in this earth age. Also by his treachery, he has been condemned already for what he has done. These are hidden truths that have to be brought out when figures of speech are used by those implying that they search for the truth. As our Lord taught in parables and was asked once to explain why he taught in parables, his answer unto his disciples was this:

Luke 8:9-10

9.   And his disciples asked him, saying, what might this parable be?

10. And he said, <u>unto you it is given to know the mysteries of the kingdom of God:</u> but to others in <u>parables; that seeing they might not see, and hearing they might not understand.</u> (KJV)

We see then that when reading scripture, we need to use common sense along with prayer, and through the Holy Spirit, we can discern the truth. The fact that a Serpent talked to Eve in the Garden should give us a clue that there is more there than just what is written, so we can have eyes to see and ears to hear. This is why there has been a lot of confusion about Satan getting into a snake, because there isn't any Scripture to substantiate this theory.

Then the tradition that the Serpent in the Garden of Eden was a snake is revealed as just that, a tradition, when you understand that the Serpent and the tree of the knowledge of good and evil are one entity. This is why the tradition that Satan got into the snake or serpent, is in error, because people could not associate the tree of the knowledge of good and evil, and the Serpent, as being one and the same.

So Christ himself affirmed that not all would understand what is spoken in Scripture. As the Holy Spirit gives understanding, it is our duty to search for truths that are in the Scriptures, and not to take every part literally, but look for the hidden meanings and truths. In the next chapter of this book, we will show what was the fruit of the tree of the knowledge of good and evil. For the traditions of men have made the Word of God of none effect.

Mark 7:13

Making the word of God of <u>none effect</u> through your tradition, which ye have delivered: and many such like things do ye. (KJV)

The words **"none effect"** has the following meaning:

208 akuroo (ak-oo-ro'-o);
from 1 (as a negative particle) and 2964; <u>to invalidate</u>:

So let your traditions go as you continue in this book and look solely at the Word of God as your only source of information. For the Scriptures is the best source of truth.

2
What Was the Fruit of the Garden of Eden?

The Tree of Life

We established in chapter 1 that Satan was the Serpent in the Garden of Eden and was also the tree of the knowledge of good and evil. Having this in mind, then we have to understand the fruit that Satan produced to cause Adam and Eve to sin. There were two different trees mentioned in Genesis. Let's start with the tree of life, which was also in the garden. This tree was denied Adam and Eve as stated in Genesis.

Gen. 3:22

> 22. And the Lord God said, Behold, the <u>man</u> is become as one of us, to know good and evil: and now, lest he put forth his hand, and take also of the <u>tree of life,</u> and eat, and live <u>for ever</u>: (KJV)

This tree would cause eternal life, as we see in the definition of forever.

5769 'owlam (o-lawm');
or 'olam (o- lawm'); from 5956; properly, concealed, i.e., the va<u>nishing point; generally, time out of mind (past or future), i.e., (practically) eternity;</u> frequentatively, adverbial (especially with the prepositional prefix) <u>always:</u>

If this tree was eternal life, then there is only one tree that could give them eternal life, and this tree was <u>Christ the Word.</u> As Satan was in the Garden of Eden, so also was our Lord and Savior Jesus Christ, <u>The Word.</u> To further document that Christ was in the garden, let's look into Genesis again.

Gen. 3:8

8. And they heard the <u>voice</u> of the Lord God <u>walking in the garden in</u> the cool of the day: and Adam and his wife hid themselves from the presence of the LORD God amongst the <u>trees of the garden</u>. (KJV)

As all Christians should know, Christ is our creator, he was God incarnate into human flesh, to lay clown his life for our sins, and was raised for our justification. This then puts our Lord and Savior in the Garden along with the Serpent (Satan).

Some have wondered why there are two different days of light and darkness mentioned in this chapter of Genesis. The first of these divisions was spiritual, and the second was a natural division. To document this we will look at the two divisions of light and darkness.

Gen. 1:3-5

3. And <u>God said,</u> Let there be light: and there was light.

4. And God saw <u>the light,</u> that it was <u>good:</u> and God divided the <u>light</u> from <u>the darkness.</u>

5. And God called the light Day, and the darkness he called Night. And the evening and the morning were the first day. (KJV)

Now this could confuse some readers. As we

read further into this chapter, we get another account of the dividing between day and night.

Gen. 1:14-19

14. And God said, Let there be <u>lights in the firmament</u> of the heaven to <u>divide the day from the night;</u> and let them be for <u>signs,</u> and for <u>seasons,</u> and for <u>days,</u> and <u>years:</u>

15. And let them be for lights in the firmament of the heaven to <u>give light upon the earth:</u> and it was so.

16. And God made <u>two great lights;</u> the <u>greater light to rule the day,</u> and the <u>lesser light to rule the night:</u> he made the stars also.

17. And God set them in the firmament of the heaven to give light upon the earth,

18. And to rule over the <u>day and over the night,</u> and to <u>divide the light from the darkness:</u> and God saw that it was good.

19. And the evening and the morning were the fourth day. (KJV)

This second division was the literal or natural division between day and night, using the creation of the sun for the day, and the moon and the starts for the night. After the throw down of Satan (the Serpent), you had one distinct division between good and evil, Christ being the good and Satan (the Serpent) the evil. Therefore God divided this earth between good and evil. It was declared by John when he wrote the following verses:

John 1:1-5

1. In the beginning was the <u>Word,</u> and the <u>Word</u> was with God, and the <u>Word was God.</u>

2. The same was in the <u>beginning with God.</u>

3. <u>All things were made by him;</u> and without him was not any thing made that was made.

4. 4n him <u>was life;</u> and the life was the <u>light of men.</u>

5. And the <u>light shineth in darkness;</u> and the <u>darkness comprehended it not.</u> (KJV)

So we see that <u>Jesus was that light that shineth in the darkness</u> and <u>Satan being evil was that darkness.</u> Then when Scripture talks about the Lord God who walked in. the Garden in the cool of the day, this was in fact Christ himself. Your <u>voice</u> is your <u>word,</u> so the voice in the Garden is also the Word, spoken of by John as being Christ. We use the words *Lord* and *God* in the same phrase, thus giving the Creator absolute authority over all things. It is interesting to note the meanings of *Lord* and *God.* The word **Lord** has the following meaning.

3068 Yehovah (yeh-ho-vaw ');
from 1961; (the) <u>self- Existent</u> or <u>Eternal;</u> Jehovah, Jewish national name of God:

The word **Yehovah** is the creator, who has <u>ALWAYS EXISTED.</u> This is why Christ could say to Moses, I AM, THAT I AM. Now we will look at the word **God.**

430 'elohiym (el-o-heem');
plural of 433; <u>gods</u> in the ordinary sense; but specifically used (in <u>the plural</u> thus, especially with the article) of the <u>supreme God;</u> occasionally applied by way of defense to magistrates; and <u>some</u>times as a <u>superlative</u>:

Here we see <u>the Godhead being plural.</u> When we look at John 1:1, we see that there was the <u>Word.</u> We also have the Holy Spirit, and God. These three, which make up the Godhead, have <u>ALWAYS BEEN IN EXISTENCE.</u> They have been the creative power behind all things created, our Father being the <u>CREATIVE MIND,</u> Christ being the <u>Word</u> that was spoken and all things were created, the Holy Spirit being the <u>POWER OF LOVE</u> between the Father, and the <u>Word,</u> which is the spirit of adoption mentioned in Romans chapter 8. This then is the Unity of the Godhead as they are united, being separated only to unite men with their creator. Notice Christ's ministry did not start until he was united with the Father in flesh and with the Holy Spirit in love. We find the following passages documenting the beginning of his ministry:

Matt. 3:15-17

15. And Jesus answering said unto him, suffer it to be so now; for thus it becometh us to <u>fulfil</u> all righteousness. Then he suffered him.

16. And <u>Jesus,</u> when he was baptized, went up straightway out of the water: and, lo, the heavens were opened unto him, and he saw the <u>Spirit of God descending like a dove, and lighting upon him:</u>

17. And lo, a <u>voice</u> from heaven, saying, <u>This is my beloved Son, in whom I am well pleased</u>. (KJV)

The word; *Word* used in John 1:1 has this meaning:

3056 logos (log'-os);
from 3004; <u>something said (including the thought);</u> by implication a topic (subject of discourse), also <u>reasoning (the mental faculty)</u> or motive; by extension, a computation; specifically (with the article in John) <u>the Divine Expression (i.e., Christ):</u>

Now *logos* being something said make <u>(Christ) the verb,</u> which is God's Creative Power. So therefore Christ as Yahovah was the Lord of the Gods. Wherefore Christ being an exact expression of God our Father inspired the writer of Hebrews to write the following:

Heb. 1:3

3. Who being the brightness of his glory, and the <u>express image</u> of his person, and upholding all things by the <u>word of his power,</u> when he had <u>by himself</u> purged our sins, <u>sat down on the right hand of the Majesty on high</u>; (KJV)

The words "**express image**," really breaks this all down. It is interesting to note that the words "**express image**" have the same meaning. You could use this as the Father and the Word.

5481 charakter (khar-ak-tare');
from the same as 5482; a graver (the tool or the person), i.e., (by implication) engraving

(["character"], the figure stamped, i.e., an exact copy or [figuratively] representation):

Here we may see an analogy of looking into a mirror and seeing oneself. This is the only way you would see an exact human copy. This is the example of what the Holy Spirit does. It reveals to us who believe, that Christ and the Father, are the exact same person. Thus was Christ in the Garden of Eden as the tree of life, being set over darkness, as Christ declared, "I am the Way, the Truth and the Life," John 14:6.+

The Fruit of the Tree

Now Eve knew the penalty of partaking of the fruit of the tree of the knowledge of good and evil, when she declared to the Serpent (Satan) what would happen if she did partake of the fruit.

Gen. 3:3

3. But of the fruit of the tree which is in the midst of the garden, God bath said, ye shall not eat of it, neither shall ye touch it, lest ye die. (KJV)

Fruit does not always mean literally fruit in Scripture. Here are some examples of the word *fruit* being used as a figure of speech. When Mary's cousin Elizabeth was talking about Mary's child that she was carrying, she used this analogy.

Luke 1:42

42. And she spake out with a loud voice, and

said, blessed art thou among women, and blessed is the <u>fruit of thy womb</u>. (KJV)

In Romans chapter 7:4- 5, Paul talks about bringing forth <u>fruit unto life,</u> and in sin we bring forth <u>fruit unto death.</u> In Gal. 5:22 he talks about the <u>fruit of the Spirit.</u> Phil 1:22 uses the phrase <u>fruit of my labor.</u> James uses this same word in James 3:18 as <u>fruit of righteousness.</u> Consequently the word *fruit* has a lot of different analogies according to how it is used. To illustrate this truth, we read in Genesis of the very sin that Satan used, to convince Adam and Eve to disobey God. He told Eve that <u>they would be as gods.</u>

How crafty and cunning is this old Serpent the Devil, and man can easily be deceived by him, if we are not rooted in God's Word. What did God actually tell <u>Adam</u> about the tree of the knowledge of good and evil, and what was the fruit of this tree?

The Different Creations

To lay the groundwork for this study, we must go back to creation and see exactly who God created, and where <u>Adam</u> fits into this picture. In Genesis we read that on the sixth day God created Man.

Gen. 1:26-27

26. And God said; Let us make man in our image, after our likeness: and let them have dominion over the fish of the sea, and over the fowl of the air, and over the cat-

tle, and over all the earth, and over every creeping thing that creepeth upon the earth.

27. So God created man in his own image, in the image of God created he him; male and female created he them. (KJV)

Let's look at the words **created** and **man**.

1254 bara' (baw-raw');
a primitive root; (absolutely) to create; (qualified) to cut down (a wood), select, feed (as formative processes): choose, create (creator), cut down, dispatch, do, make (fat).

What does the word *Adam* actually mean in the Hebrew? We think of it only as a name, but in reality it has a real meaning.

120 'adam (aw-dawm');
from 119; ruddy i.e., a human being (an individual or the species, mankind, etc.):
KJV—X another, + hypocrite, + common sort, X low, man (mean, of low degree), person.

As we look at the meanings of this word **Adam**, there are a lot of hidden facts described therein. This Adam, who was created on the sixth day, signifies the ones whom we will show in later chapters, used hypocritically, demeaned and put into bondage, their goods plundered, to control mankind. Now The Adam formed on a later day, has this meaning.

119 'adam (aw-dam');
to show blood (in the face), i.e., flush or turn rosy: KJV—be (dyed, made) red (ruddy).

It is our belief that 119 is from 120, for the definition of 120 is the creative work that God did on the sixth day. This makes 119 that which was formed at a later time. Could this have been a cover- up by those who translated the Scripture, to keep the fact that there were others on this earth when Adam was formed? More on the cover- up in Scripture in chapter 4. To further document that there were others on this earth at this time, we read the following account in Genesis:

Gen. 2:1

1. Thus the heavens and the earth <u>were finished,</u> and all the <u>host</u> of them. (KJV)

What does ***host*** mean? We see that God's creation was finished with all the host of them.

6635 tsaba' (tsaw-baw');
or (feminine) tseba'ah (tseb- aw- aw'); from 6633; <u>a mass of persons</u> (or figuratively, things), especially reg. organized for war <u>(an army);</u> by implication, a campaign, literally or figuratively (specifically, hardship, worship): KJV—appointed time, (+) army, (+) battle, <u>company, host,</u> service, <u>soldiers,</u> waiting upon, war (- fare).

With these meanings of host, Scripture clearly shows there were a lot of people <u>created</u> at the finish of the sixth day. Looking back at the meaning of Adam closely, we see that Adam is an individual or a species of mankind. Then Adam is not all of mankind, but a part of it. Then all <u>humans</u> who were called Adam were created on the sixth day. <u>The Adam</u> formed after the day God rested, appears to be on a different day. Now the Hebrew word used in the manuscripts before the formed Adam is <u>Haa,</u> which is <u>The.</u> So the text reads <u>The Adam</u> was <u>formed,</u> which is different from Adam created. This account is written in Genesis:

Gen. 2:7

7. And the Lord God <u>formed man</u> of the dust of the ground, and breathed into his nostrils the breath of life; and man became a living soul. (KJV)

The word *formed* has the following meaning.

3335 yatsar (yaw-tsar');
probably identical with 3334 (through the <u>squeezing into shape); (</u>[compare 3331]); <u>to mould into a form;</u> especially as a potter; figuratively, to determine (i.e., form a resolution):

So the manuscripts clearly show that <u>The Adam</u> is the nationalities of people who show blood in the face or to put it more clearer, they were of fair complexion.

The Fruit of the Tree

Looking now into what God told Adam of the Tree of the Knowledge of Good and Evil, we find a different account of what Eve told Satan.

Gen. 2:16-17

16. And the Lord God commanded the man, saying, Of every tree of the garden thou mayest freely eat:

17. But of the tree of the knowledge of good and evil, thou shalt <u>not eat</u> of it: for in the

day that thou eatest thereof thou <u>shalt</u> surely die. (KJV)

God commanded Adam not to eat of the tree. In essence he actually told Adam not to partake of this knowledge, to leave this tree alone completely. Now Eve took this a little bit further, as we see in the following account.

Gen. 3:3-4

3. But of the fruit of the tree which is in the midst of the garden, God hath said, ye shall not eat of it, neither shall ye <u>touch it, lest ye die.</u>

4. And the serpent said unto the woman, <u>Ye shall not surely die</u>: (KJV)

What Eve did then was to add touch to God's statement. This word *touch* will be dealt with in the chapter 3. So what was the fruit of the tree of the knowledge of good and evil?

It was Satan's deception that they would be as <u>gods.</u> This would make them <u>gods over all the other people of this earth.</u> Thus their eyes were opened to the physical differences between the people of this earth. This is the big lie that has led others of Satan's seed to think that they are gods and to lord over other peoples of this planet. This was the original teaching of racism, which is a false doctrine, contrived by the Serpent. We will show in subsequent chapters that the word *race* is only used as in running in a race or in competition. It is never applied to mankind as a species.

Although he said they would surely die, we

know that they lived a long time after this happened, but what God was saying, meant spiritual as well as a natural death. But the point is when you believe Satan and his lies and follow his direction; you will die spiritually and in the end be destroyed. How simple is the truth of God's Word, when we look into the spiritual, and not the natural things of God's truths. As stated in Ephesians,

Eph. 6:12

12. For we wrestle not against <u>flesh and blood,</u> but against <u>principalities, against powers, against the rulers of the darkness of this world, against spiritual wickedness in high places</u>. (KJV)

So to take the fruit as an apple, or other such fruit would be foolish, as we are in a spiritual war. God said that we should "Love the Lord thy God and only him should you serve," <u>"love your neighbor as yourself."</u> Any other is sin against our Father. This is how <u>traditions</u> of man can make <u>void</u> or of <u>non-effect</u> the truth of God's Word. In the next chapter, we will explore more in depth the results of this fruit that Eve did partake of.

3
What Is the Genealogy of Cain?
The Encounter of Eve with the Serpent (Satan)

This is the heart of this book, and when we conclude this chapter, it is the authors' desire that you will come away with a fresh new outlook on Scripture such as you have never had before. The common theological belief is that Cain was the firstborn of Adam. If you take Scripture at face value, you can come to this conclusion. Let's dig deeper into God's Word and discover more hidden meanings that you may have never looked into before.

Let's go into Eve's first encounter with the Serpent (Satan) in the Garden of Eden. In the biblical account of Genesis 3, we read the following.

Gen. 3:2-3

2. And the woman said unto the serpent. We may eat of the fruit of the trees of the garden:

3. But of the fruit of the tree which is in the midst of the garden, God hath said, ye shall not eat of it, neither <u>shall ye touch</u> it, lest ye die. (KJV)

Remember in the last chapter we mentioned the subject, that Eve added <u>touch</u> to God's commandment. Continuing on, God gave Adam permission to eat of all the trees except for the tree in the midst of the garden. In verse 3 we will look very closely at the words <u>shall ye touch?</u> According to *Strong's Exhaustive Concordance,* we find the following meaning.

5060 nags' (naw-gah');
a primitive root; properly, <u>to touch,</u> i.e., lays the hand upon (for any purpose; euphem. <u>to lie with a woman);</u> by implication, to reach (figuratively, to arrive, acquire); violently, to strike (punish, defeat, destroy, etc.):

Having this in mind, let's look at *Vine's Expository Dictionary* to get another view of the word ***touch***.

TOUCH, TO
Naga' first occurs in < Gen. 3:3> in the Garden of Eden story where the woman reminds the serpent that God had said: "Ye shall not eat of [the fruit of the tree which is in the midst of the garden]; neither shall ye touch it..." "This illustrates the common meaning of <u>physical touch</u> involving various kinds of objects: <u>Jacob's thigh was "touched" by the man at Jabbok</u>
< Gen. 32:25, 32>
(from *Vine's Expository Dictionary of Biblical Words)*
(Copyright © 1985. Thomas Nelson Publishers)

Here a picture is being painted that indicates not only physical touch, as indicated in *Vine's* definition, <u>but in Strong's we see the euphemism "to lie with a woman."</u> From chapter 1 a euphemism was defined as using a <u>less direct phrase or word for an offensive one.</u> This will probably offend a lot of students of God's Word as you are thinking that these authors are trying to say that Satan had physical contact with Eve, with a sexual connotation involved. Well, if you will just bear with us, we will go into Scripture a little further and explain how we came to this conclusion.

Going into the Genesis account of Eve's encounter with the Serpent, we will attempt to clear up the misunderstandings of what actually took place.

Gen. 3:6

6. And when the woman saw that the tree was good for <u>food,</u> and that it was <u>pleasant</u> to the eyes, and a tree to be <u>desired</u> to make one wise, she took of the fruit thereof, and did eat, and <u>gave also unto her husband</u> with her; and he did eat. (KJV)

The word *food* means literal or figurative food. But we have been seeing that figures of speech have been used in earlier Scripture, so let's continue to take a closer look for understanding. We have used these figures of speech in our daily lives such as; "food for thought," "food for the soul." So the word **food** does not always mean actual food for your mouth or stomach. Looking at the word in this verse, which is pleasant, you will find another meaning added to Eve's statement.

Now most food is pleasant to the eye when you are hungry, but in *Strong's,* we get this meaning.

2530 chamad (khaw-mad');
a primitive root; <u>to delight in:</u> KJV—<u>beauty,</u>

greatly beloved, covet, delectable thing, (X great) delight, desire, goodly, lust, (be) pleasant (thing), precious (thing).

Now we are talking about the Serpent or Satan as this tree, and we know that he was created according to Ezekiel 28:12, full of wisdom, and perfect in beauty. We remember in chapter 1, that the word *tree* is a figure of speech for body. We also read in the first chapter, from Ezekiel chapter 31, documenting the Serpent (Satan) as a tree of the knowledge of good and evil. So the Serpent or Satan was one of the most beautiful of God's creations, and would attract any mortal person. For it goes on to say in this verse, "a tree to be desired to make one wise." The word *desire* has the following meanings.

8378 ta'avah (tah-av-aw');
from 183 (abbreviated); a longing; by implication, a delight (subjectively, satisfaction, objectively, a charm):
KJV—dainty, desire, X exceedingly, X greedily, lust (ing), pleasant. See also 6914

What we have here is this beautiful person whom God created, very appealing to look at, and desirable to the eye. The word *desire* also means charm, so the Serpent (Satan) was charming.

We also see in the KJV, that this word is used as meaning greedily, lust(ing). His words were also full of wisdom, which were hard for a woman or anyone for that matter to resist. We are dealing with a supernatural being, who is far beyond anything that a mere mortal could understand.

This debunks the theory of Satan having horns and a tail and looking grotesque. To further substantiate how we reached this conclusion, reading further in verse 6, you will notice that Eve gave to Adam and he also did eat. Now, was Adam there when this happened, or as it appears in later verses, that what Eve did was to tell Adam what really happened, and he ate, or better yet absorbed the knowledge that <u>Eve gave him</u>? We have used the word **"eat"** as a figure of speech, i.e., "When he was in class, he ate up all the knowledge he could absorb." The reason why we use the word "eat" as a figure of speech is that the next verse makes more sense.

Gen. 3:7

7. <u>And the eyes of them both were opened,</u> and <u>they knew</u> that they were <u>naked;</u> and they <u>sewed fig leaves together,</u> and made themselves aprons. (KJV)

Verse 7 says <u>"And the eyes of both were opened,</u> and <u>they knew they were naked."</u> If there was not a sexual encounter with the Serpent, and Eve ate only a piece of fruit, and gave that fruit to Adam to eat, then what would make them know that they were <u>naked?</u>

The question then arises; did Adam have a sexual involvement with the Serpent as Eve did? No, because we read in 1 Timothy.

1 Tim. 2:14

14. And <u>Adam was not deceived,</u> but the woman <u>being deceived </u>was in the transgression. (KJV)

The meaning of *deceived* is as follows

538 apatao (ap-at-ah'-o);
of uncertain derivation; to cheat, i.e., delude:

Now the meaning of *cheat* and *delude,* according to the *American Heritage Dictionary:* First **cheat.**

1. To <u>deceive by trickery;</u> swindle: cheated customers by overcharging them for purchases.
2. To <u>deprive by trickery; defraud:</u> cheated them of their land.
3. To <u>mislead;</u> fool: illusions that cheat the eye.

Look at the meaning of **delude.**

1. <u>To receive the mind or judgment</u> of: fraudulent ads that delude consumers into sending in money. See Synonyms at DECEIVE.
2. Obsolete. To elude or evade.
3. Obsolete. To frustrate <u>the hopes </u>or <u>plans</u> of.

Shocking as this may seem, Adam's sin was honoring his wife, more than honoring God's Word (Christ). Not leaving his wife when she sinned, but going along with her encounter with the Serpent, Adam was brought into the same snare. Also remember that the Serpent promised them they <u>would be as gods,</u> which is a little more than just knowledge. Why did they cover themselves with fig leaves?

Knowledge of Nakedness

Now what knowledge did they receive from the Serpent making them know they were naked? There is an interesting thought put forth in Genesis 3:20 after their encounter with God, when Adam called his wife Eve "the mother of all living." This was before Adam knew his wife (sexually). We will now look at what happened when God and Adam had a conversation concerning Eve's encounter with Serpent.

Gen. 3:10-16

10. And he said, I heard thy voice in the garden, and I was afraid, because <u>I was naked;</u> and <u>I hid myself.</u>

11. And he said, <u>who told thee that thou wast naked?</u> Hast thou <u>eaten</u> of the <u>tree,</u> whereof I commanded thee that thou shouldest <u>not eat?</u>

12. And the man said, the <u>woman</u> whom thou gayest to be with me, she <u>gave me of the tree,</u> and I <u>did eat.</u>

13. And the Lord God said unto the woman, what is this that thou hast done? And the woman said, the serpent <u>beguiled</u> me, and I did eat.

14. And the <u>LORD God said unto the serpent,</u> Because thou hast done this, thou art cursed above all cattle, and above every beast of the field; upon thy belly shalt thou go, and dust shalt thou eat all the days of thy life:

15. And I will put enmity between thee and

the woman, and <u>between thy seed and her seed;</u> it shall bruise thy head, and thou shalt bruise his heel.

16. Unto the woman he said, <u>I will greatly multiply thy sorrow and thy conception; in sorrow thou shalt bring forth children; and thy desire shall be to thy husband, and he shall rule over thee.</u>

In this conversation we see what really happened between Eve and the Serpent. In verse 11 God asked Adam how did he know he was naked. Did he partake of the knowledge? Partake is a synonym for eat, so Adam did eat or believe the knowledge Eve had received. When Adam told God that it was Eve who fed him this knowledge that they were naked, God then asked Eve what she did.

Eve's Seed and Satan's Seed

In verse 13 Eve told God that the Serpent "beguiled me, and I did eat." The word **beguiled** in the Hebrew has the following meaning.

5377 nasha' (naw-shaw');
a primitive root; to lead astray, i.e., <u>(mentally) to delude, or (morally) to seduce:</u>

In Corinthians Paul fully understands what took place and gives this account of what took place.

2 Cor. 11:3

3. But I fear, lest by any means, as the serpent <u>beguiled</u> Eve through his subtilty, so

your minds should be corrupted from the simplicity that is in Christ. (KJV)

Now the word **beguiles** in the Greek means this:

1818 exapatao (ex-ap-at-ah'o);
from 1537 and 538; <u>to seduce wholly:</u>

So in the Greek we see that "beguile" means; to seduce wholly. This meant a <u>total seduction,</u> "wholly," <u>Exapatao</u> in the Greek is where we get our word *espouse* from, which means to wed. What Paul describes here is a total seduction of Eve, and warns the Corinthians, who had a fornication problem, that there would be leaders who would even create other gospels in order to take control of their flocks.

With these meanings in mind, we will go further in the verses of Genesis. In verse 14, we read that the Serpent was cursed to eat the dust. Earlier we discussed this, as a figure of speech, showing that man was made from dust, that the Serpent (Satan) was accountable for all the souls that he deceived, and is condemned to die for his deception. Verse 15 talks about the Serpent's seed and Eve's seed. Seed has the following meaning.

2233 zera' (zeh'-rah);
from 2232; seed; figuratively, fruit plant, sowing- time, <u>posterity:</u>

We see that <u>seed</u> has several meanings, but the one that seems to apply is <u>posterity.</u> Now if the Serpent (Satan) had seed, then who is it? Also who was Eve's seed? How could the Serpent (Satan) possibly have a seed? As previously stated, that seed was posterity, or better understood as our line of children. If the Serpent (Satan) had a line, then the only seed that could be from the Serpent is Cain.

The statement "I will put <u>enmity</u> between thee and the women, and between <u>thy seed</u> and <u>her seed;</u> it shall bruise thy head, and thou shalt bruise his heel,' ' was a twofold prophetic promise. We know that Cain killed Abel, which was the immediate enmity prophesied by God between the seeds. This meant hostility between the two, which is what enmity means. It also goes down through history to Christ himself, where Satan's seed killed Christ to try to end the Messiah ship. To this day there is still hatred by the Serpent's (Satan) seed for the heirs in Christ. Thus we see that in the end, Satan will be destroyed by Christ, as he was the second part of this prophetic statement.

This also explains why God told Eve in verse 16: <u>"I will greatly multiply thy sorrow and thy conception; in sorrow thou shalt bring forth children; and thy desire shall be to thy husband and he shall rule over thee."</u> This encounter between Eve and the Serpent (Satan), really got God's anger up, making child bearing a hard thing for women. Also this is why Christ said that adultery was the only grounds for divorce. God also put adultery in its own prohibitory commandment.

The Birth of Cain and Abel

If you are still holding onto your traditions

and reading along with us in these verses, you could say, Well, Eve said that when she bore Cain "I got a man from the Lord." Let's look at this verse and see the account of the birth of Cain and Abel.

Gen. 4:1-2

1. And Adam knew Eve his wife; and she conceived; and <u>bare Cain,</u> and said, I have gotten a man from the <u>LORD.</u>

2. And she <u>again</u> bare his <u>brother Abel.</u> And Abel was a <u>keeper of sheep,</u> but Cain was a <u>tiller of the ground.</u> (KJV)

Eve stated in verse 1 that when she bore Cain she had gotten a man from the Lord. The word **Lord** in the Bible is Yahovah (3068) in *Strong's.* We believe that this statement here, of God being the father of Cain is a contradiction within itself. We feel the <u>Kenites,</u> whom you will learn more about in the next two chapters, have substituted Yahovah instead of the Serpent being the father of Cain. Further documentation, which shows that the Serpent is the father, is in Matthew as spoken by Jesus himself.

Matt. 13:38-39

38. The field is the world; the good seed are the children of the kingdom; but the <u>tares are the children of the wicked one:</u>

39. <u>The enemy that sowed them is the devil;</u> the harvest is the end of the world; and the reapers are the angels. (KJV)

To further document that Cain was the Serpent's son, we read in 1 John the following:

1 John 3:12

10. Not as <u>Cain, who was of that wicked one,</u> and slew his brother. And wherefore slew he him? Because <u>his own works were evil,</u> and his brother's righteous. (KJV)

God could not have given Eve a murderer for a child. It is our opinion that she was referring not to the Creator, or our God, but to her Lord Satan, whom she had given in to. Satan, then became the Lord of man. This is why Jesus himself had to be born of the Holy Spirit, so sin could not be found in him. This brings to mind the saying of Jesus when he said,

Matt. 12:33

33. Either <u>makes the tree good, and his fruit good;</u> or else makes the <u>tree corrupt, and his fruit corrupt; for the tree is known by his fruit</u>. (KJV)

In this statement, Jesus was referring to himself and Satan as the trees. We are all sinners at birth, but it took the death and resurrection of our Lord Jesus Christ to recover us, and redeem our souls from sure death.

Now if we look at the birth of Cain and Abel, we will see a startling revelation, for when it says "she <u>again</u> bares his brother Abel," the word *again* has hidden the reality concerning Cain and Abel's birth, that they were twins.

3254 yacaph (yaw-saf');
a primitive root; to add or <u>augment</u> (often adverbial, <u>to continue to do a thing):</u>

In *Vine's Expository Dictionary* the word **yacap** has these meanings.

yacap3254, "to add, <u>continue, do again,</u> surpass." This verb occurs in the northwest Semitic dialects and Aramaic. It occurs in biblical Hebrew (around 210 times), post- biblical Hebrew, and in biblical Aramic (once).
(from *Vine's Expository Dictionary of Biblical Words)* (Copyright © 1985, Thomas Nelson Publishers)

There is another verse in which the word **<u>again</u>** is used, but with a different word and meaning.

Gen. 4:25

25. And Adam knew his wife <u>again;</u> and she bares a son, and called his name Seth: For God, said she, hath appointed me another seed instead of Abel, whom Cain slew. (KJV)

The meaning of "again" in this verse is different.

5750 'owd (ode);
or 'od (ode); from 5749; properly, <u>iteration or continuance;</u> used only adverbially (with or without preposition), <u>again,</u> repeatedly, still, more:

So what it really says is that she <u>continued in labor</u> and had Abel. This makes Cain and Abel twins. You could look at all this and ask; how could this be possible for a woman to have twins from two different fathers? This is a common occurrence in the case of <u>fraternal twins.</u> Let's see the meaning of fraternal.

Biology. Of, relating to, or being a twin developed from <u>two separately fertilized ova;</u> dizygotic.

They are from two different eggs in a woman. This could be accomplished with two different encounters with the male. <u>Identical twins</u> are from the same egg, which splits. Looking into *identical,* we find the following meaning.

Biology. Of or relating to a twin or twins developed from the <u>same fertilized ovum</u> and having the same genetic makeup and closely similar appearance; monozygotic.

Therefore this is what happened, that they were fraternal twins, because they were from two different male sperms. We will talk more about how Satan produced seed in the next chapter. To further prove this point, we will look at the genealogy of Adam. You will see that Cain is not mentioned. Cain has his own genealogy, which is separate from Adam's, because he was not Adam's son. For your benefit and comparison, here is a brief list of Cain's and Adam's genealogies.

Gen. 4:16-22

16. And Cain went out from the presence of the Lord, and dwelt in the land of Nod, on the east of Eden.

17. And Cain knew his wife; and she conceived, and bare Enoch: and he builded a city, and called the name of the city, after the name of his son, Enoch.

18. And unto Enoch was born had: and Irad begat Mehujael: and Mehujael begat Methusael: and Methusael begat Lamech.

19. And Lamech took unto him two wives: the name of the one was Adah, and the name of the other Zillah.

20. And Adah bare Jabel: he was the father of such as dwell in tents, and of such as have cattle.

21. And his brother's name was Jubal: he was the father of all such as handle the harp and organ.

22. And Zillah, she also bare Tubalcain, an instructer - of every artificer in brass and iron: and the sister of Tubalcain was Naamah. (KJV)

The following is the **genealogy of Adam:**

Gen. 5:1-32

1. This is the book of the generations of Adam. In the day that God created man, in the likeness of God made he him;

2. Male and female created he them; and blessed them, and called their name Adam, in the day when they were created.

3. And Adam lived an hundred and thirty years, and begat a son in his own likeness, after his image; and called his name Seth:

4. And the days of Adam after he had begotten Seth were eight hundred years: and he begat sons and daughters:

5. And all the days that Adam lived were nine hundred and thirty years: and he died.

6. And Seth lived an hundred and five years, and begat Enos:

7. And Seth lived after he begat Enos eight hundred and seven years, and begat sons and daughters:

8. And all the days of Seth were nine hundred and twelve years: and he died. And Noah was five hundred years old: and Noah begat Shem, Ham, and Japheth. (KJV)

The authors know that this will shock a lot of readers, and might anger a lot of scholars. This book is to plant seed, and in prayer we will let the Holy Spirit give the understanding. If these writings do nothing more than make a person search the Scriptures to check out what we are saying, and in deep prayer look for the truth, then we have accomplished our goals.

The next chapter will deal with the sons of Cain, whose name in the Bible is <u>Kenites,</u> which means the <u>Sons of Cain.</u> Where were they throughout history, and how did they survive the Flood of Noah? We will also get into why these truths are not clear in Scripture.

4
What Role Did the Kenites (Sons of Cain) Play in Biblical History?

The Kenites are mentioned throughout the Old Testament, and our Lord Jesus Christ mentioned them when he spake to the scribes and Pharisees. To prove that Kenite means sons of Cain, we will look at the meaning in the Hebrew concerning the word **Kenit**e.

> **7017 Qeyniy (kay-nee');**
> or Oiyniy (1 Chron. 2:55) (kee- nee'); patronymic from 7014; a Kenite or member of the tribe of Kajin: KJV—Kenite.

We will now look at the 7014 to see the prime root of this word.

> **7014 Oayin (kah' -yin);**
> the same as 7013 (with a play upon the affinity to 7069); Kajin, the name of the first child, also of a place in Palestine, and of an Oriental tribe: KJV—Cain, Kenite (- s).

When looking up the meanings for Kenite, we found that in Numbers 24:22 the meaning was that of 7014. Now in all other verses where Kenite was mentioned, the 7017 definition was used as the meaning. We would also point out that this was another cover- up of Satan's seed to disguise themselves, as the letter K is used instead of C, to mislead you away from their true identity. To show that Cain and Kenite have the same affiliation, the word *affinity* has these specific meanings.

1. A <u>natural attraction</u> or feeling of fellowship.
2. <u>Relationship by marriage.</u>
3. An inherent similarity between persons or things. See Synonyms at <u>LIKENESS.</u>

In these meanings we can link up the word **Kenites** with Cain as being the first child. We know that Cain went to the land of Nod, which may be located in Asia, therefore his tribe perhaps being of Oriental background. To find out more about this background, there is another definition from the *Browns Driver and Briggs Concordance,* which defines Kenites thus.

7014 Oayin-
as a proper noun, masculine: <u>Cain</u> = "possession";
1. the oldest son of Adam and Eve and the first murderer having murdered his brother Abel
2. as a proper noun, <u>gentilic;</u> Kenite = "smiths"; the tribe from which the father-in-law of Moses was a member and which lived in the area between southern Palestine and the mountains of Sinai.

As we digest this meaning, we will see an interesting fact brought out here. Preceding 2), we read that this word is a proper noun, <u>gentilic.</u> <u>Gentilic.</u> This is just another way of saying Gentile. This confirms the fact that Cain was not blood-related to Adam, because in Adam's genealogy we have the Semitic nationalities, which we call non- Gentile.

A note to the readers: because Cain may have ended up in Asia in the land of Nod, we do not imply that Asians are Kenites.

A note of history: during World War II Goebbels had his propaganda headquarters located in a town called <u>Kenitesburg,</u> Germany.

Why is all this so important, you might say? Well, being the seed of Satan (Serpent), this group of people has throughout history tried to thwart God's plan to save the world through our Savior Jesus Christ. Now we know there are some who will say that any seed of Satan (Serpent) would have been destroyed in the Flood, as all living flesh was destroyed except Noah and his family, plus two of all the animals. If we look deep into the Word of God, we will find out how what we state could happen, and how these angelic beings took wives and sired children.

The Days of Noah, the Sons of God, and the Flood

To enlighten us on this subject, we will go to Genesis and look at the story of **Noah**.

Gen. 6:1-2

1. And it came to pass, when <u>men</u> began to multiply on the face of the earth, and daughters were born unto them,

2. That the <u>sons of God</u> saw the daughters of men that they were fair; and they took them wives of all which they chose. (KJV)

The sons of God were not mortal men. We find throughout Scripture, that when God was talking to any human, he referred to him as a son of man. This also applied to Christ himself when he was on earth, in a human body. To further document that the sons of God were angelic beings, we turn to the Book of Job.

Job 1:6

6.   Now there was a day when the <u>sons of God</u> came to <u>present</u> themselves before the LORD, and <u>Satan came also among them</u>. (KJV)

This not only shows that angelic beings were the <u>sons of God,</u> but we also see that Satan, or the Serpent as he is sometimes called, was also with them as a son of God, for he was the first created. So the sons of God were angelic beings sent down here by Satan to pollute the line that Jesus was to come through, to stop God from the fulfillment of prophecy, made by God to the Serpent and Eve.

The First Throw down of Satan

We know that Satan (Lucifer) deceived at least a third of the angels, to follow him before his throw down, which was in the world that existed before this earth age. Documentation for this is found in Revelation.

Rev. 12:3-4

3.   And there appeared another wonder in heaven; and behold a <u>great red dragon,</u> having <u>seven heads and ten horns, and seven crowns upon his heads.</u>

4. And his <u>tail drew the third part of the stars of heaven,</u> and did cast them to the earth: and the <u>dragon stood before the woman which was ready to be delivered, for to devour her child as soon as it was born</u>. (KJV)

The word **dragon** has a distinct meaning in the Greek.

1404 drakon (drak'-own);
probably from an alternate form of derkomai (to look); <u>a fabulous kind of serpent (perhaps as supposed to fascinate):</u>

Here we see the Serpent at work, in the world that then was, when he drew a third part of the angels to him, as stars are referred to as angels in verse 4. To further document that stars are referred to as angels, we read the following in Revelation.

Rev. 1:20

20. The mystery of the seven <u>stars which thou sawest in my right hand,</u> and the seven golden candlesticks. The seven <u>stars are the angels</u> of the seven churches: and the seven candlesticks which thou sawest are the seven churches. (KJV)

We will show in a later chapter that those stars, being angels, will be thrown out of heaven with that old Serpent the Devil, which will be his second overthrow.

When God punished Eve (Gen 3:16) and Satan for their encounter in the Garden of Eden, Satan became aware of God's prophetic judgment, that the Messiah was going to come into this world through a woman, to destroy his kingdom. To document that Christ would come through a woman; we will go to Paul's writing in 1 Timothy:

1 Tim. 2:14-15

14. And Adam was not deceived, but the woman being deceived was in the transgression.

15. Notwithstanding <u>she shall be saved in childbearing,</u> if <u>they</u> continue in faith and charity and holiness with sobriety. (KJV)

In reading the manuscripts, we found that the phrase "she shall be saved in childbearing" is misleading. This appears to be speaking to childbearing in general. Looking into the manuscripts, it was very specific that it referred only to one child, which was Christ, being born through a woman. The word "they" was not in the manuscripts. It really translates to "abide or remain." This does not in any way say that women through childbirth would be saved, as this verse indicates. If that were true, then what would happen to a woman who could not bear any children?

Because the Serpent (Satan) sowed the evil tares in the field (Matt. 13:39), he was condemned to death. This may anger a lot of scholars, but we will show that Paul in the Book of Romans, explained why God allowed <u>the beguilement of Eve</u> in the Garden of Eden, to give God the justification for the destruction of the Serpent.

Rom. 8:20-22

20. For the <u>creature</u> was made <u>subject to vanity, not willingly,</u> but by reason of him who hath <u>subjected the same in hope,</u>

21. Because the creature itself also shall be <u>delivered from the bondage of corruption into the glorious liberty of the children of God.</u>

22. <u>For we know that the whole creation groaneth and travaileth in pain together until now</u>. (KJV)

What Paul was referring to is that man was subject to vanity. The word *vanity* has the following meaning in the Greek:

3153 mataiotes (mat-ah-yot'-ace);
from 3152; <u>inutility</u> figuratively, transientness; <u>morally, depravity:</u>

Paul is saying in this verse that man was made useless, morally depraved, but not because the creature was willing, but because it was God's plan to destroy Satan. If Adam and Eve had not sinned, then they would have lived forever, thus so would Satan. By God allowing the beguilement of Eve, as the Serpent had sown his seed into mankind, it laid the foundation for God to do likewise with the birth of Jesus Christ, which would then be the latter fulfillment of the prophecy God gave to Eve and the Serpent: "he shalt bruise your head and thou shall bruise his heel."

Paul goes on further in these verses to say

that through Christ we have hope and through him and in him, there is eternal life. This is why God chose a virgin for Christ to be born through by the use of the sexual process, without being exposed to human corruption, but through the power of the Holy Spirit, making Christ the literal offspring of God.

In Verse 4 we see that the Serpent (Satan) was waiting for Christ to be born, so he could have him put to death. We also know the end of this story, as Christ did defeat Satan and took him back to heaven when he ascended. The fact that the angels were of a male heritage, is the reason why we believe that these were the stars or angels in Genesis, who had the encounter with the daughters of men.

Gen. 6:2

2. That the sons of <u>God</u> saw the daughters of men that they were fair; and <u>they took them wives</u> of all which they chose. (KJV)

When the Serpent (Satan) knew that Christ or the Messiah would come to destroy him, we believe he then sent these angelic beings down to earth to pollute the daughters of men that Christ would descend through. Therefore the taking of wives meant a sexual encounter with the daughters of men. We see the results of these angels coming in unto the daughters of men.

Gen. 6:4

4. There were <u>giants</u> in the earth in those days; and also after that, when the sons of God came in unto the daughters of <u>men,</u> and <u>they bare children</u> to them, the same

became mighty <u>men which</u> were of <u>old men</u> of renown. (KJV)

The word **_giants_** in the Hebrew has the following meaning.

5303 nephiyl (nef-eel');
or nephil (nef- eel'); from 5307; properly, a <u>feller,</u> i.e. a <u>bully or tyrant:</u>

There is an interesting note to this word, that the definite article is used before nephiyl, making the meaning, <u>the nephiyl.</u> Now you would think that God would have destroyed these beings in the Flood of Noah. If God had destroyed all flesh except Noah and his family, then how could they have survived the Flood, and still been mentioned again in the Book of Numbers? When the children of Israel first came to the promised land, they found giants in the land.

Num. 13:32-33

32. And they brought up an evil report of the land which they had searched unto the children of Israel saying, The land, through which we have gone to search it, is a land that eateth up the inhabitants thereof; and all the people that we saw in it are men of a great stature.

33. And there we saw the <u>giants,</u> the sons of Anak, which come of the giants: and we were in our own sight as grasshoppers, and so we were in their sight. (KJV)

This is a startling find, as the Nephiylim mentioned in Genesis now appear in the promised land. This explains why Goliath being a giant, was there, he whom the shepherd David killed with his sling.

Proof of the Existence of the Different Nationalities

This now brings us to the point of answering the question of where did all the nationalities come from, and did they exist before the Flood? If they did exist, how did they survive the Flood? Is there proof that the Kenites changed Scripture to cover up the fact that the different nationalities were created on the sixth day?

We find the word *men* are used three times in Genesis 6:4. The first use of the **word *men* is translated into Adam.**

120 'adam (aw-dawm');
from 119; ruddy i.e., <u>a human being (an individual or the species, mankind,</u> etc.):
KJV—X <u>another,</u> + <u>hypocrite, + common sort, X low, man (mean, of low degree), person.</u>

It is interesting to see that Adam does mean a human being, but also a species. Note what the King James's people provided in other translations of Adam, as <u>another,</u> a hypocrite or <u>common sort, a person of low degree.</u> We will see in chapter 5 why the Kenites have used the Adamic people as a scapegoat for their evil ways, to put the blame on Adam. Going into 119 we find a different Adam.

119 'adam (aw-dam');
to show blood (in the face), i.e., flush or turn rosy:

There is a difference in spelling, making this a different Adam.

Here is a description of the characteristics of the offspring of sons of God. Does this sound like some leaders in our world today? The meaning for mighty is:

1368 gibbowr (ghib-bore';
or (shortened) gibbor (ghib- bore'); intensive from the same as 1397; powerful; by implication, warrior, tyrant:

By this definition we can see why these offspring were not in the interest of God's plan for men. Now going into the men of renown, we get a different meaning for men.

376 'iysh (eesh);
contracted for 582 [or perhaps rather from an unused root meaning to be exant]; a man as an individual or a male person; often used as an adjunct to a more definite term (and in such cases frequently not expressed in translation):

Looking into this definition of man, there is a word in this meaning that stands out. This word is **extant,** which according to the *American Heritage Dictionary* has this meaning.

1.   Still in existence; not destroyed, lost, or extinct: extant manuscripts.

2.   Archaic. Standing out; projecting.

So men were still in existence. To further show the existence of a fourth man, we will look at the meaning of 582.

582 'enowsh (en-oshe');
from 605; properly, a <u>mortal (and thus differ-ing from the more dignified 120);</u> hence, a man in general (singly or collectively):

Here in this meaning, it is an admission that there were other men, but their bias shows through when it is stated that 120 or <u>The Adam</u> of 119 is more dignified. We will show in chapter 5 why this attitude was adopted. So we have four different nationalities of men in *iysh, enowsh, adam,* and the *aadam.* We also would like to point out Ezekiel 31, where different kinds of trees were used in the Garden of Eden to denote different people.

Remember this is pre- Flood and four differ-ent men are mentioned here. Now if those of Sa-tan's angels could sire children, then so could Satan himself. We know by reading in Genesis 6:12- 13 that God was distressed with what hap-pened and decided to destroy all that had the breath of life, but to keep two of each species to repopulate the earth. This is the flood spoken of by Peter when he said:

2 Pet. 2:5

5. And <u>spared not the old world, but saved Noah the eighth</u> person, a preacher of righteousness, bringing in the flood upon the world of the ungodly; (KJV)

This is Noah's Flood. Going into the manu-scripts, we will find the wording a little different.

And old world not spared but <u>eighth No-ah</u> of righteousness a preacher was <u>saved</u>

Noah was not the eighth from Adam but the tenth in line. Eight in biblical numerics means, "resurrection, regeneration, also a new beginning or commencement." The word **saved** has a significant meaning in the Greek.

5442 phulasso (foo-las'-so);
probably from 5443 through the idea of isolation; to watch, i.e., be on guard (literally or figuratively); by implication, to preserve, obey, avoid:

So Noah was found righteous because he was on guard and kept watch over that which God had commanded to men. He found favor in God's sight because he humbled himself to God. Although Noah was not perfect—we know that he got drunk after the Flood—he still found grace in God's sight.

The Separating of Noah's Flood and the World That Then Was

Now here is where some confusion sets in, because what Peter was talking about was Noah's Flood in chapter 2. When he gets into the flood in chapter 3, it is commonly believed that this is the continuance of the Flood of Noah. This is not true. He is talking about the throw down of Satan, and the destruction of the world that then was.

2 Pet. 3:3-6

3. Knowing this first, that there shall come in the last days scoffers, walking after their own lusts,

4. And saying, Where is the promise of his coming? for since the fathers fell asleep, all things continue as they were from the <u>beginning of the creation.</u>

5. For this <u>they willingly are ignorant</u> of, that by the word of God the heavens were of old, and the earth standing out of the water and in the water:

6. Whereby the <u>world that then was,</u> being <u>overflowed with wa</u>ter, <u>perished</u>: (KJV)

Very 3 clearly shows this is end- time prophecy. When Peter writes in chapter 3, he was admonishing the church, concerning the teachings of Jesus about the angels returning in the end time.

The End Times Concerning Noah and the Return of Those Angels

Matt. 24:37-39

37. But as the <u>days of Noe</u> were, so shall <u>also</u> the coming of the Son of man

38. For as in the days that were <u>before the flood they</u> were eating and drinking, <u>marrying and giving in marriage,</u> until the day that Noe entered into the ark,

39. And knew not until <u>the flood</u> came, and took them all away; so shall also the <u>coming of the Son of man be</u>. (KJV)

The significance of people giving and taking in marriage would be of no revelation, but when you understand that this is talking about the angels in those days, this is critical to the understanding to the Christians, especially when you hear of genetic engineering.

This correlates along with Jude in his epistle warning them about the same account of these angels coming back.

Jude 1:3

3.	Beloved, when I <u>gave all diligence</u> to write unto you of the common salvation, it was needful for me to write unto you, and exhort you that ye should earnestly contend for the <u>faith which was once delivered</u> unto the saints. (KJV)

In the above verse, Jude was addressing the believers concerning their teachings that only consisted of salvation. When looking at the manuscripts, we found that what Jude also told them, was to make haste, to get away from the teachings that those who had crept in were holding back from the believers, which was that the doctrine concerning those angels who left their first estate during the time of Noah <u>had to be taught.</u>

Jude 1:6

6.	And <u>the angels which kept not their first estate,</u> but left their own habitation, he hath restored in everlasting chains under darkness unto the judgment of the great day. (KJV)

So the reference in 2 Peter chapter 3 was not about Noah's Flood, but the overthrow of Lucifer (Satan) and his angels, in the world that then was, which was destroyed in the gap between

Genesis 1:1 and 1:2. Here we see that the Kenites, by changing the meanings of old in both cases, giving the illusion that Noah's Flood in chapter 2 is older than the account of the flood in chapter 3, switching those meanings.

We would like to take a look at the meaning of the word *old* used in both chapters. We have two different meanings for the word **old** used in each of these references. First in 2 Peter 2:5, the word *old* has this meaning.

744 archaios (ar-khah'-yos);
from 746; <u>original or primeval:</u>

Going into the root word of this, we get the following meaning:

746 arche (ar-khay');
from 756; (properly abstract) a <u>commencement,</u> or (concretely) chief (in various applications of order, time, place, or rank): KJV— <u>beginning,</u> corner, (at the, the) first (estate), magistrate, power, principality, principle, rule.

Now in 2 Peter 3:5, the word *old is* rendered in this manner:

1597 ekpalai (eh'-pal-ahee);
from 1537 and 3819; <u>long ago,</u> for a long while:

This shows that the meanings were switched, which is why we can understand why some scholars could be confused when looking at these different meanings, not understanding the origins of the Kenites, and their agenda of not being discovered. This was the overthrow of Satan or the Serpent and is confirmed in the gap between Genesis 1:1 and 1:2.

Noah's Flood

Now the question still lingers, were only Noah and his family saved during the Flood of his time? We will look into Scripture to see what actually did take place.

Gen. 6:18-21

18. But with thee will I establish my covenant; and thou shalt come into the ark, <u>thou, and thy sons, and thy wife, and thy sons' wives with thee.</u>

19. And of <u>every living thing of all flesh,</u> two of every sort shalt thou bring into the ark, to keep them alive with thee; they shall be <u>male</u> and female.

20. Of fowls after their kind, and of cattle after their kind, of every creeping thing of the earth after his kind, two of every sort shall come unto thee, to keep them alive.

21. And take thou unto thee of all food that is eaten, and thou shalt gather it to thee; and it shall be for food for thee, and for them.

To rightly divide the Word of God, let's go into the meanings of these verses. As we look at verse 18, it clearly states that Noah and his sons, and his wife, and their wives would be saved. Looking into verse 19, this story will get clearer as we look into the real meanings of various words. The words "and of every" mean, <u>whole or all.</u> The phrase **"living"** has the following meaning.

2416 chay (khah'-ee);
from 2421; <u>alive;</u> hence, <u>raw (flesh);</u> fresh
(plant, water, year), strong; also (as noun, especially in the feminine singular and masculine
plural) life <u>(or living thing),</u> whether <u>literally or
figuratively:</u>

Look at the word *flesh* to get a real insight
into what God was saying.

1320 basar (baw-sawr');
from 1319; flesh (from its freshness); by extension, <u>body, person;</u> also (by <u>euphem,) the
pudenda of a man:</u>
KJV—body, [fat, lean] <u>flesh [- ed],</u> kin, [man-]
kind, + nakednesself, skin.

What are **pudenda** and how does this definition fit into these meanings? Let's see what the
American Heritage Dictionary has to say.

The human external genitalia, <u>especially of a
woman.</u> Often used in the plural.

Keeping <u>two men and women</u> of all flesh,
even their genitals. These meanings cannot be
talking about animals that went aboard the ark,
but human beings or <u>Mankind</u> by two, which
were on the ark. The word *"chat",* is also the
word that was translated "beast" in Genesis 3:1
referring to the Serpent in that passage of Scripture.

Where the misunderstanding comes is in
verse 20 when God refers to birds, cattle, and
creeping things. This sounds like it only means
animals that went into the ark, with Noah, and
his family, until you read the next portion, which
states "two of all (whole) shall come unto thee, to

keep them alive." The word **sort** was added by the translators. So if you read this verse correctly, it will include <u>all living beings were saved.</u> This is why we have our different nationalities of people today, as they were saved during the Flood and dispersed after the waters receded.

Archaeologists have found ancient ruins, going back to the time before Abraham, which tell of *a* great deluge that covered the earth. Most all ancient cultures speak of this deluge. Where could these stories come from, if it had not actually happened, and people survived the flood? The accounts given by these ancient cultures coincide with the biblical account of the Flood. When we read Genesis chapter 10, we find in verse 5 that it declares, the Gentiles had to be on the ark with Noah and his sons.

Gen. 10:1-6

1. Now these are the generations of the sons of Noah, Shem, Ham, and Japheth: and unto them were sons born after the flood.

2. The sons of Japheth; Gomer, and Magog, and Madai, and Javan, and Tubal, and Meshech, and Tiras.

3. And the sons of Gomer; Ashkenaz, and Riphath, and Togarmah.

4. And the sons of Javan; Elishah, and Tarshish, Kittim, and Dodanim.

5. By these were <u>the isles of the Gentiles</u> divided in their lands; every one <u>after his tongue,</u> after their families, in their nations.

6. And the sons of Ham; Cush, and Mizraim, and Phut, and Canaan. (KJV)

Looking at verse 5, some will say that this is before the Tower of Babel, so how could they speak different tongues? The explanation is a simple one. If you look at people in these United States, who all basically speak English, we sometimes still have a problem understanding those from different parts of our country. For example people from the South use different sounds and pronunciations than people from the North and even in the western parts. So, all the different nationalities entered in with Noah and his offsprings to be saved on the ark.

To further document we will reiterate what we said in an earlier chapter, that there were others created is verified in Genesis chapter 2.

Gen. 2:1

1. Thus the heavens and the earth were <u>finished,</u> and all the <u>host </u>of them. (KJV)

What we see in this verse are two key words. The first is *finished*, which has the following meaning.

3615 kalah (kaw-law');
a primitive root; to end, whether intransitive <u>(to cease, be finished, </u>perish) or transitived <u>(to complete,</u> prepare, consume):

Now when God completed his restoration of heavens and earth, he told those he created to <u>replenish</u> the earth. He now uses the word *host*. To look at the word **host** again to show that this meaning still applies.

6635 tsaba' (tsaw-baw');
or (feminine) tseba'ah (tseb- aw- aw'); from 6633; <u>a mass of persons</u> (or figuratively, things), especially reg. organized for war <u>(army);</u> by implication, a campaign, literally or figuratively (specifically, hardship, worship):

This verse is talking about a <u>host</u> of people, not just Adam, who had not been formed as yet. To further document this, going into the Hebrew manuscripts, the word used for *host* is "ts ab-aa'amm." The last part of this word, <u>amm,</u> is not connected with the meaning *host,* but has a different meaning to it.

5971 'am (am);
from 6004; <u>a people</u> (as <u>a congregated unit);</u> <u>specifically, a tribe (</u>as those of Israel); hence (collectively) troops or attendants; figuratively, a flock:
KJV—folk, men, <u>nation, people.</u>

This word being in the plural is talking about a host of different people that were created on the sixth day. A further study of the word ***created,*** looking into Genesis when "he created man in his image."

1254 bara' (baw-raw');
a primitive root; <u>(absolutely) to create;</u> (qualified) to cut down (a wood), select, feed (as formative processes): <u>- choose, create (creator),</u> cut down, dispatch, do, make (fat).

This word is an absolute act, creating something out of nothing, which is what God did when he originally created this earth. After God created man, he formed Adam, Genesis 2:7. Now the word *form* as stated before, is quite different from created.

3335 yatsar (yaw-tsar');
probably identical with 3334 (through the squeezing into shape); ([compare 3331]); to mould into a form; especially as a potter; figuratively, to determine (i.e., form a resolution):

Here God is shaping as if using clay like a potter. We know that Adam means red or ruddy, which is the type of clay God used to form man. Adam was just a name of the man formed. When Cain went off to the land of Nod, there were people living there. Where did these people come from? There are indications that Noah had Asiatic features. To document further on Adam, let's read what Paul says about Adam.

1 Cor. 15:45

> 45. And so it is written, The first man Adam was made a living soul; the last Adam was made a quickening spirit. (KJV)

Knowing that Christ was not the last man, as there have been many men who were born after Christ, this is just a figure of speech for the Adamic people. As Adam was the first, then Christ was the last. We will see in later chapters that after Christ's death, the Gentiles would be grafted onto the vine, which is Christ. So Adam was not in reality the first man.

The word *race* is mentioned four times in the Bible: Psalms 19:5, Ecclesiastes 9:11, 1 Corinthians 9:24, and Hebrews: 12:1. In all cases the word did not refer to a nationality of people, but of running a race. If God does not refer to people as races, then why do we? The word *race* was not used for people, until the Greeks used it for the purpose of dividing and conquering different peoples.

Kenites

We can see in several passages of Scriptures that the Kenites are mentioned. The first time is in Genesis.

Gen. 15:18-19

18. In the same day the LORD made a covenant with Abram, saying, Unto thy seed have I given this land, from the river of Egypt unto the great river, the river Euphrates:

19. The Kenites, and the Kenizzites, and the Kadmonites, (KJV)

In other verses they are mentioned also. This was all after the Flood.

In **Baalam's** prophecies he stated the following:

Num. 24:21-22

21. And he looked on the Kenites, and took up his parable, and said, Strong is thy dwelling place, and thou puttest thy nest in a rock.

22. Nevertheless the Kenite shall be wasted, until Asshur shall carry thee away captive. (KJV)

This verse has a lot of meanings, but we will not go into them at this time. You can search these meanings for yourself.

The Kenites are mentioned in the following verses: Judges 4:11, 1 Samuel 15:6, 27:10, 30:29. We are sure that the reader at this point is asking why are we spending so much time and devoting a full chapter to the Kenites. The importance of the Kenites is in their origin as sons of Cain, who were the children of the Serpent (Satan), which has been hidden in Scripture.

There are many who will say that men of God sat down and wrote the Scriptures and it is literally true, except when we see <u>who did some of the translating of Scripture</u> and how Satan has used his own, to cover up his true identity. Shocking as this may seem, the Kenites have altered some of the translations to keep the average reader <u>unaware</u> of the Kenites' true identity and purposes. Can we prove this startling statement? Yes. Let's look into 1 Chronicles, and we will get a picture of how the Kenites got into the position to change the understanding of certain Scriptures, and cover up who they are.

1 Chron. 2:55

> 55. And the families of the <u>scribes</u> which dwelt at Jabez; the Tyirathites, the Shimeathites, and Suchathites. These are the <u>Keni</u>tes that came of Hemath, the father of the house of <u>Rechab.</u> (KJV)

Here we see what the Kenites' occupation was. They were the <u>scribes.</u> The scribes were the ones who kept the records of all the writings. Our Lord Jesus Christ knew exactly who they were when he addressed them in Matthew.

Matt. 23:1-2

1.   Then spake Jesus to the multitude, and to his disciples,

2.   Saying, <u>The scribes and the Pharisees sit in Moses' seat</u>: (KJV)

We see that Christ knew that the scribes had a lot of power, as they sat in the seat of Moses, which left them the power to translate Scripture as they saw fit. Further in Scripture, in the Book of John, Christ further explains who these scribes really were and who was their father.

John 8:39-44

39.   They answered and said unto him, <u>Abraham is our father.</u> Jesus saith unto them, If <u>ye were Abraham's children, ye would do the works of Abraham.</u>

40.   But now <u>ye seek to kill me,</u> a man that hath told you the truth, which I have heard of God: <u>this did not Abraham.</u>

41.   <u>Ye do the deeds of your father.</u> Then said they to him, <u>We be not born of fornication; we have one Father, even God.</u>

42.   Jesus said unto them, <u>If God were your Father, ye would love</u> me: for I proceeded forth and came from God; neither came I of myself, but he sent me.

43.   Why do ye not understand my speech? <u>even because ye cannot hear my word.</u>

44.   <u>Ye are of your father the devil, and the lusts of your father ye will do. He was a murderer from the beginning,</u> and <u>abode</u>

not in the truth, because there is no truth in him. When he speaketh a lie, he speaketh of his own; for he is liar, and the father of it. (KJV)

This tells it all. We see in verse 39 that the Kenites claimed to be of Abraham. This will be covered in a later chapter, when we go into the Church and the Great Tribulation, where it states that there are those who claim to be of Judah and are not (Rev. chapters 2 and 3). In verse 40 Jesus states that they were the ones who were trying to kill our Lord.

Our brother Judah has been falsely accused for the problems that have happened, even to the crucifying of our Lord, when it was the Kenites who were the ones who actually did the false accusation, which led to his death on the cross.

We note that in verse 41 that they knew that Cain was born out of wedlock, but they were trying to deny this, as they said, they were not born of fornication. They also claim God as their father, but in verse 42, Jesus makes a statement that "if God were your Father, ye would love me."

We know that God created all of mankind, but the Kenites' alliance was not with God but of their Father the Devil. This is explained in verse 44 when Christ says exactly who they are, and what they have to do. He then goes into their genealogy when he says, "he was a murder from the beginning." Who was the first murderer mentioned in the Bible? When we look at the definition of Cain in the first part of this chapter, we find that the first murderer was Cain.

Then Cain being the Serpent (Satan's) son, and his offspring called Kenites were the scribes even in Christ's day, <u>Jesus referred to them concerning their true identity.</u> For further definitions that declare what Jesus said about the scribes, read Matthew chapter 23.

Now we know that Satan is a liar and the father of lies, then he will keep this a secret from the average person as to who his family is and their plan to stop God's plan from coming to fulfillment. It was the Scribes and Pharisees who had Christ nailed on the cross, so their father Satan (Devil) could try and stop the Messiah from doing his mission, of saving us from destruction. As we know this failed because God is All in All and in control of all things. There are events that he allows, to bring forth his glory, but in the end as believers, we will overcome, if we stay in God's Word, and put it in our minds that we might not sin against him.

Kenites and the Church Today

There are those who have followed this book so far and will say, well, maybe there is some truth in what we have written, but this all ended when Jesus died on the cross and arose out of the tomb, defeating Satan and conquering death, hell, and the grave. This is another lie that Satan is tempting God's people into believing, that all is all right now, and we do not have to fight every day and study to show ourselves approved unto God. Paul said it well in Timothy.

2 Tim. 2:15

15. <u>Study to shew thyself approved unto God,</u>

a workman that needeth not to be ashamed, <u>rightly dividing</u> the word of truth. (KJV)

In Jude we can see happenings not only in the church in the apostles' time, but relevant to our times today.

Jude 1:4-6

4. For there are <u>certain men crept in unawares, who were before of old ordained to this condemnation,</u> ungodly men, turning the grace of our God into lasciviousness, and denying the only Lord God, and our Lord Jesus Christ.

5. I will therefore put you in remembrance, <u>though ye once knew this,</u> how that the Lord, having saved the people out of the land of Egypt, afterward destroyed them that believed not.

6. <u>And the angels which kept not their first estate, but left their own habitation,</u> he bath reserved in everlasting chains under darkness unto the judgment of the great day. (KJV)

The first few words, Jude tells us what is happening in the Church of his day, and it is more important in these last days. The words **"crept in unawares"** have a special meaning.

3921 pareisduno (par-ice-doo'-no);
from 3844 and a compound of 1519 and 1416; to <u>settle in alongside,</u> i.e., lodge <u>stealthily:</u>

As in Jude's day, we have those who have crept in unawares or as the meaning says settled in alongside. They promulgate traditions that are not in accordance with the truth of God's Word. The word *stealthily* reminds us of our Stealth Bombers, which are supposed to fly to their target without being detected.

As we look at verse 4 a little more, we see the phrase "who were before of old ordained to this condemnation." The word <u>old</u> has this meaning.

3819 palai (pal'-ahee);
probably another form for 3825 (through the idea of <u>retrocession);</u> (adverbially) <u>formerly,</u> or (by relatively) sometime since; (elliptically as adjective) <u>ancient:</u>
KJV—any while, <u>a great while ago, (of) old, in-time past.</u>

These are the angels who remain as they were, from the beginning of creation, and kept in the same state at the time of their fall.

It is up to each and every believer to make him or herself aware by digging into the Word of God and searching out the truth. Not relying only on someone to explain what this or that means, but checking it out for yourselves.

These Kenites will stop at nothing to distort the Word of God and bring it to non- effect, by using traditions and false teachings to keep the body of Christ from the truth. We also see a confirmation that the sons of God who came down and married were angels, when in verse 6 Jude talks about the angels who left their first estate, which was heaven. The Apostle Paul said it well when he writes in Romans.

Rom. 15:4

4.   For whatsoever things were written afore-

time were written for our learning, that we through patience and comfort of the scriptures might have hope.(KJV)

In verses 11- 13 of Jude, we will see what the Kenites can do to those who are not armed with the whole armor of God and know not the truth of God's word.

Jude 1:11-13

11. Woe unto them! for they have gone in the <u>way of Cain,</u> and ran greedily after the error of Balaam for reward, and perished in the gainsaying of Core.

12. These are <u>spots</u> in your feasts of charity, when they feast with you, feeding themselves without fear: clouds they are without water, carried about of winds; <u>trees whose fruit withereth, without fruit, twice dead,</u> plucked up by the roots;

13. Raging waters of the sea, foaming out their own shame; wandering stars, to whom is reserved the blackness of darkness for ever. (KJV)

The first part of verse 11 should prove that the Kenites who are of Cain are well and operating in the body of Christ, not only in Jude's time, but more so in these last days when Satan's about to appear on the scene as Antichrist. The *American Heritage Dictionary* defines **anti** as follows.

1. a. <u>Opposite:</u> antimere. b. Opposing; against: antiapartheid. c. Counteracting; neutralizing: antibody.

2. Inverse: antilogarithm.

Looking at the meaning of *inverse*, we can clearly see Satan's role.

1. Reversed in order, nature, or effect.

So Satan is a reverse in the order of Christ, who has to come first, before our Lord can appear on the scene. He also opposes and is against all that is righteous and good. All unrighteousness comes from Satan. We will get more into the Second Coming in a later chapter. In verse 12 we see that they are spots in your feast of charity.

You have heard the expression that a leopard cannot change his spots. Well, the leopard in Daniel is Satan's children, the Kenites. So then the spots in Jude are from Satan's children and will sneak in stealthily to mislead the Body of Christ. Examples of this are lack of compassion, little or no charity for the poor. As the Scripture says, "by their fruits you shall know them" (Matt. 7:20).

Let us quote the last part of this chapter for the edification of the Body of Christ and may the Lord Jesus Christ through his Holy Spirit bless you as you read what will happen in the end times.

Jude 1:17-25

17. But, beloved, remember ye the words which were spoken before of the apostles of our Lord Jesus Christ;

18. How that they told you there should be mockers in the last time, who should walk

after their own ungodly lusts.

19. These be they who separate themselves, sensual, having not the Spirit.

20. But ye, beloved, building up yourselves on your most holy faith, praying in the Holy Ghost.

21. Keep yourselves in the lover of God, looking for the mercy of our Lord Jesus Christ unto eternal life.

22. And of some have compassion, making a difference:

23. And others save with fear, pulling them out of the fire; hating even the garment spotted by the flesh.

24. Now unto him that is able to keep you from falling, and to present you faultless before the presence of his glory with exceeding joy,

25. To the only wise God our Savior, be glory and majesty, dominion and power, both now and ever. Amen. (KJV)

What we have revealed in this chapter is that Satan has done his best to disguise his purpose, even to the extent of distorting some of the translations of the Bible, so the average reader would be unaware of who is trying to steal away your rewards in Christ, by letting his children creep into our basic beliefs and letting us believe more in our traditions than in the Word of God. Jesus put it better than we could when he condemned the false teachers in Matthew.

Matt. 7:21-23

21. <u>Not every one that saith unto me, Lord, Lord, shall enter into the kingdom of heaven;</u> but he that <u>doeth the will of my Father</u> which is in heaven.

22. Many will say to me <u>in that day, Lord, Lord,</u> have <u>we not prophesied</u> in thy name? and in thy name have <u>cast out devils?</u> and in thy name <u>done many wonderful works?</u>

23. And then <u>will I profess unto them, I never knew you:</u> depart from me, ye that work iniquity. (KJV)

These are powerful Scriptures for those who think that they are professing the right doctrine, in Jesus' name, but are going after the traditions of men and not the real truth of God's Word.

We are not saying that all teachers of God's Word are Kenites or that the Bible is completely mistranslated. But there are false teachers, and there are parts of Scripture which if you check out the original meanings through a *Strong's Exhaustive Concordance* or a good computer Bible study, you will find several parts where the translations are poorly done as to the original meanings that were intended to be understood.

In the next chapter, we will see how the Kenites have come on the world scene and changed things, to eventually set up Satan's one-world system.

5
The High Cabal and the
New World Order
The High Cabal

Today many Americans as well as the world at large can remember when President George Bush proclaimed to the world the introduction of the New World Order. Books have been written on this subject, but what really did this mean, and what impact will it have on us in the future? To clarify this we have to look at the High Cabal. What does Scripture have to say about this High Cabal and what is it?

In Matthew chapter 13, we will see what Scripture has to say concerning the Cabal.

Matt. 13:34-35

34. All these things spake Jesus unto the multitude in parables; and without a parable spake he not unto them:

35. That it might be fulfilled which was spo-ken by the prophet, saying, I will open my mouth in parables; I will utter things which have been kept secret from the foundation of the world. (KJV)

Now let's look at the words underlined to find out their meanings.

2928 krupto (kroop'-to); a primary verb; to conceal (properly, by covering): KJV—hide (self), keep secret, secret [- ly].

Lucifer's (Great Red Dragon) Original Throw down

The word **krupto** is where we get our word **crypto**, which is used for secrecy. This is what Satan and his seed, the Kenites, have attempted to do, creating the confusion in Genesis chapter 1; concerning Lucifer's (the great red dragon) throw down in the world that then was (Rev. 12:3- 4). Normally, most secret organizations are tied into the Cabal, which requires a secret oath of silence, keeping one bound to their concept of secrecy. Now let's look at the meaning of the word *foundation.*

2602 katabole (kat-ab-ol-ay ');
from *2598;* a <u>deposition,</u> i.e., founding; figuratively, conception:

Going into the root of this word, we get another meaning.

2598 <u>kataballo</u> (kat-ab-al'-lo);
from 2596 and 906; to throw down:

Now as we look at the word *foundation,* you see the word **katabole,** which is Cabal in the English. It is interesting to note that the root word <u>katabole</u> is to throw down. When did this throw down take place, and why? Who was the prophet whom the Scripture was referring to, when and where was this prophecy conceived? Let's go into Isaiah and find the implication of this prophecy.

Isa. 6:1-3

1. In the year that king Uzziah died <u>I saw also the Lord sitting upon a throne,</u> high

and lifted up, and <u>his train filled the temple.</u>

2. Above it stood the seraphims: each one had six wings; with twain he covered his face, and with twain he covered his feet, and with twain he did fly.

3. And one cried unto another, and said, Holy, holy, holy, is the <u>LORD</u> of hosts: <u>the whole earth is full of his glory</u>. (KJV)

This vision that Isaiah saw was the Lord, sitting on his throne. Where was his throne located? In Heaven? No! It was on earth as we look at verse 3 and see that "the whole earth is full of his glory." The only meaning that can be derived from this, that this happened in the <u>World That Then Was</u> or also referred to as the First Earth Age. This was before the fall of Lucifer. To further document this, we will go to 2 Peter.

2 Pet. 3:3-6

3. Knowing this first, that there shall cone in the <u>last days scoff</u>ers, walking after their own lusts,

4. And saying, <u>Where is the promise of his coming?</u> for since the fathers fell asleep, all things continue as they were <u>from the beginning of the creation.</u>

5. For this they <u>willingly</u> are <u>ignorant</u> of, that by the word of God the heavens were of old, and <u>the earth standing out of the water and in the water:</u>

6. Whereby the <u>world that then was,</u> being overflowed with water, <u>perished:</u> (KJV)

Interestingly the phrase "willingly are ignorant" simply implies that you have first-hand
knowledge. Paul explains in Romans:

Rom. 1:20-21

20. For the <u>invisible things of him from the
    creation</u> of the world <u>are clearly seen, be-
    ing understood</u> by the things that are
    made, even his eternal power and God-
    head; so that they are <u>without excuse:</u>

21. Because that, <u>when they knew God, they
    glorified him not as God, neither were
    thankful;</u> but <u>became vain in their imagi-
    nations,</u> and their foolish heart was dark-
    ened

This meaning of the <u>word **knew** is an absolute knowledge of.</u>

1097 ginosko (ghin-oce'ko);
a prolonged form of a primary verb; <u>to "know"
(absolutely)</u> in a great variety of applications
and with many implications (as follow, with
others not thus clearly expressed):
KJV—allow, <u>be aware (of),</u> feel, (have) <u>know (-
ledge), perceived, be resolved,</u> can speak, be
sure, <u>understand.</u>

These were the angels who did not follow
God, but fell with Lucifer in the throw down or
kataballo. Note that verse 21 when it says that
when they "knew God, they glorified him not."
When did they know God, except in the world
that then was? Let's look at verse 6 of 2 Peter
chapter 3, going into the word **perished.**

622 apollumi (ap-ol'-loo-mee);

from 575 and the base of 3639; <u>to destroy fully.</u> (reflexively, to <u>perish,</u> or lose), literally or figuratively:

Isaiah talked about Lucifer before his overthrow in these passages of Scripture:

Isa. 14:12-19

12. <u>How art thou fallen from heaven, 0 Lucifer, son of the morning! how art thou cut down to the ground, which didst weaken the nations!</u>

13. For thou hast <u>said in thine heart, I will ascend into heaven, I will exact my throne above the stars of God; I will sit also upon the mount of the congregation, in the sides of the north:</u>

14. <u>I will ascend above the heights of the clouds; I will be like the most High.</u>

15. Yet <u>thou shalt be brought down to hell, to the sides of the pit.</u>

16. They that see thee shall narrowly look upon thee, and consider thee, saying, Is this <u>the man</u> that made the earth to tremble, that did shake kingdoms;

17. That made the world as a wilderness, and destroyed the cities thereof; that opened not the house of his prisoners?

18. All the kings of the nations, even all of them, lie in glory, every one in his own house.

19. <u>But thou art cast out of the grave like an abominable branch,</u> and as the raiment of

those that are slain, thrust through with a sword, that go down to the stones of the pit; as a carcase trodden under feet. (KJV)

To further document the throw down of Satan or Lucifer in the world that then was, we will refer to Ezekiel and see what the prophet had to say about Lucifer's fall.

Ezek. 28:13-17

13. Thou <u>has been in Eden the garden of God;</u> every precious stone was thy covering, the sardius, topaz, and the diamond, the beryl, the onyx, and the jasper, the sapphire, the emerald, and the carbuncle, and gold: the workmanship of thy tabrets and of thy pipes was prepared in thee in the day that thou wast <u>created.</u>

14. Thou art the <u>anointed cherub</u> that covereth; and I have set thee so: thou wast upon the holy mountain of God; thou hast walked up and down in the midst of the stones of fire.

15. Thou wast perfect in thy ways from the day that thou wast created, till iniquity was found in thee.

16. By the multitude of thy <u>merchandise</u> they have filled the midst of thee with violence, and thou hast sinned: therefore I will <u>cast</u> thee as profane out of the mountain of God: and I will destroy thee, <u>0 covering cherub,</u> from the midst of the stones of fire.

17. 1Thine heart was lifted up because of thy beauty; thou hast corrupted thy wisdom

by reason of thy brightness: I will <u>cast thee</u> to the ground; I will lay thee before kings, that they may behold thee. (KJV)

The words ***cast thee*** have the following meaning:

7993 shalak (shaw-lak);
a primitive root; <u>to throw out, down or away (literally or figuratively)</u>

It is interesting to note that before his overthrow, the one whom we now know as Satan, was called Lucifer. After he was cast down, he became known as Satan, the Serpent, etc. The idea that he was the Serpent in the garden shows that some time had to have elapsed because he is now called the Serpent and no longer Lucifer.

In Peter he was talking about the complete destruction of the heavens of old and the earth of old, while here in Ezekiel the prophet describes Satan as an Anointed Cherub before sin was found in his heart. In essence God was revealing in his Word, the whole picture through the prophets Ezekiel and Isaiah, and through Peter and Paul. All was perfect in the world that then was, until Lucifer sinned and God destroyed that heaven and earth. To further document this, we will go to Genesis.

Gen. 1:1-2

1. In the beginning God <u>created</u> the <u>heaven</u> and the earth.

2. And the earth was <u>without form,</u> and <u>void;</u> and darkness was upon the face of the deep. And the Spirit of God moved upon

the face of the waters. (KJV)

There is a gap between verses 1 and 2. To document this gap, we will look at the word created in verse 1.

1254 tiara' (baw-raw');
a primitive root; (absolutely) to create; (qualified) to cut down (a wood), select, feed (as formative processes): - choose, create (creator), cut down, dispatch, do, make (fat).

We can see that create or creator is used in this word, and it has a meaning of absolutely to create. This means that there was nothing in existence before the Godhead created the heaven and the earth. Now let's look at verse 2 and the meaning of without form, and void.

8414 tohuw (to'-hoo);
from an unused root meaning to lie waste; a desolation (or surface), i.e., desert; figuratively, a worthless thing; adverbially, in vain:

This first meaning of *without form* could not be used in verse 1 of Genesis because created is past tense; the order of things were completed. Now *void* has the following meaning.

922 bohuw (bo'-hoo);
from an unused root (meaning to be empty); a vacuity, i.e., (superficially) an undistinguishable ruin:

It is the authors' belief that the Godhead did make a decision when Lucifer or Satan sinned and took a third part of the stars, or angels with him, whether he should destroy the earth or the people or both. It is our belief that God decided to destroy just the earth, and divide the heavens to place the souls there, to be sent back to this earth age again, without any knowledge of what had taken place prior to the overthrow. This is why we can only use a portion of our brain. We feel that those who are found worthy and are changed at the return of Christ, will have their brains restored to their original state. God would then send Christ to go through this earth age for our salvation.

To show that the Godhead made no exceptions to this rule, that all had to pass through this earth age, the Godhead passed through this earth in form and person of our Lord Jesus Christ. Documentation is found in the following verses:

John 1:10

10. He was in the world, and the world was made by him, and the world knew him not. (KJV)

Col. 2:9

9. For in him dwelleth all the fullness of the Godhead bodily. (KJV)

This is why the angels mentioned in Jude are locked in a chain of circumstances, not being able to pass through this earth age or be born again. Then all who pass through this earth age have had the opportunity for salvation.

The Dividing of the Heaven

To document the dividing of the heavens, we

will go further in Genesis.

Gen. 2:1

1. Thus the <u>heavens</u> and the earth were fin-
    ished, and all the <u>host</u> of them. (KJV)

So we see that here the heavens are plural,
which is different from Genesis 1:1 in which it is
heaven, which is singular. Also in Genesis, we
read the following.

Gen. 1:28

28. And God blessed them, and God said unto
    them, Be fruitful, and multiply, and <u>re-
    plenish</u> the earth, and subdue it; and have
    dominion over the fish of the sea, and over
    the fowl of the air, and over every living
    thing that moveth upon the earth. (KJV)

Then reading in verse 28 in which God says
for man to <u>replenish</u> the earth, what was he saying? We know that you cannot replenish what
was not there before. To further document this,
let's go to Jeremiah.

Jer. 4:23-27

23. I beheld the earth, and, lo, it was <u>without
    form, and void;</u> and the heavens, and they
    had no light.

24. I beheld the mountains, and, lo, they
    trembled, and all the hills moved lightly.

25. I beheld, and, lo, there was no man, and all
    the birds of the heavens were fled.

26. I beheld, and, lo, the fruitful place was a

wilderness, and all the cities thereof were broken down at the presence of the LORD, and by his fierce anger.

27. For thus hath the LORD said, <u>The whole land shall be desolate; yet will I not make a full end</u>. (KJV)

What Jeremiah saw was the "world that then was" or "the first earth age" destroyed by God. In verse 1 we see the word *heavens* (plural), which was the same as in Genesis, thus documenting that he did divide the heaven at Lucifer or Satan's throw-down. Also there was complete darkness on the earth. This means that Satan is darkness and so is sin. It wasn't until God separated the light (Christ) from darkness (Satan) that this world was ready to be replenished.

In verse 27 God says that he will not make <u>a full end.</u> Therefore God will use this earth, until he brings down the New Heaven and New Earth, which is going to be dealt with in a later chapter. It is amazing that he even saw cities that were destroyed.

We are going to quote Isaiah 6:8-12 to further show that he, Isaiah, was in the world that then was, and volunteered to be sent to this earth.

Isa. 6:8-12

8. Also I heard the voice of the Lord, saying, <u>Whom shall I send, and who will go for us? Then said I, Here am I; send me.</u>

9. And he said, Go, and tell this people, Hear ye indeed, but understand not; and see ye indeed, but perceive not.

10. Make the heart of this people fat, and make their ears heavy, and shut their eyes; lest they see with their eyes, and hear with their ears, and understand with their heart, and convert, and be healed.

11. Then said I, Lord, <u>how long?</u> And he answered, <u>Until the cities be wasted without inhabitant, and the houses without man, and the land be utterly desolate,</u>

12. And the Lord have <u>removed men far away,</u> and there <u>be a great forsaking in the midst of the land</u>. (KJV)

As we read in verse 3 of this chapter, the earth was filled with his glory. This could only happen before the throw down of Lucifer. When Isaiah asked how long before he would go, the answer was very precise in verse 11. This also coincides with what Jeremiah saw when he looked back and saw that the earth was desolation.

Why We Have the Problems We Do on This Earth

Now for a little history on why we have the troubles that have caused the dividing of our people. Why can nationalities not seem to co-exist? Is this the way God planned our world to be? Not hardly, as we were all created in his image. But events of our history, which we believe have been planned by Satan to divide us from God, have transpired to make what we now know as the alienation of our different nationalities, such as the division of color, standard of living, education, et cetera.

The High Cabal

Since mankind first inhabited this earth, there have been wars and squabbling among different peoples, but nothing like what we see today. As far back as 2,000 years ago in ancient Chinese history, during the time of the emperors and the various dynasties, there was a secret group that controlled the affairs of men, whom they called the High Cabal. Interestingly enough, in Chinese architecture and mythology, the Dragon, Lion, and Serpent are generally portrayed.

But our real trouble started when Ferdinand Magellan went on an expedition and when his crew reported back to Spain that the world was a sphere instead of being flat. It was Magellan's belief that he could sail completely around the world and his crew proved it. Now the bankers of Antwerp in Brussels, Belgium, heard of his theory and knew that if this was true, then the earth was finite and had limited resources. They saw this as a way to acquire the riches of the world, if they could claim these resources for themselves. This put these men in line with what Ezekiel saw of Satan who wanted all the riches in the world that then was.

Ezek. 28:4-5

4. With thy wisdom and <u>with thine understanding</u> thou hast gotten thee riches, and hast gotten gold and silver into thy treas-

ures:

5. By thy great wisdom and by thy <u>traffick</u> hast thou increased thy <u>riches,</u> and thine heart is lifted up because of thy <u>riches:</u> (KJV)

As we read these verses, the word **under-standing** seems to stand out. The Hebrew meaning for the word *understanding* also includes the words **"with thine,"** which is actually one word.

8394 tabuwn (taw-boon');
and (feminine) tebuwnah (teb- oo- naw'); or towbunah (to- boonaw'); from 995; <u>intelligence;</u> by implication, <u>an argument;</u> by extension, <u>ca-price:</u>

It is interesting to look at the meaning of *ca-price,* which means, <u>"a sudden, impulsive change in thinking or acting."</u> This sudden change in our thinking concerning the peoples of this earth is what has caused the problems that befall this world.

Satan, in changing his mind about what God wanted done and only looking at himself and his desires and aims to control the riches of this world, <u>transferred this idea into his offspring, the Kenites.</u> Looking at the word *traffick,* we get the idea why there is so much greed in this world.

7404 rekullah (rek-ool-law');
feminine passive participle of 7402; <u>trade (as peddled):</u> KJW—merchandise, traffic.

Going to the prime root of this word, we have a little clearer understanding.

7402 rakal (raw-kal');
a primitive root; to <u>travel for trading:</u> KJV—(spice) <u>merchant.</u>

It is greed and the desire of control over this earth, and having all the wealth, and making the rest of the world poor and destitute. This is why our Lord Jesus Christ would say in Matthew the following:

Matt. 6:24

24. No man can serve two masters: for either he will <u>hate the one,</u> and <u>love the other;</u> or else he will <u>hold to the one,</u> and <u>despise the other.</u> Ye <u>cannot serve God and mammon.</u> (KJV)

The word *mammon* has been controversial in meaning, but there is only one meaning and that is wealth and the greed to acquire this wealth.

3126 mamonas (mam-o-nas') or mammonas (mam-mo-nas');
of Aramaic origin (confidence, i.e., <u>wealth, personified);</u> mammonas, i.e., <u>avarice (deified):</u>

Here is wealth personified. Also the word *avarice* has this meaning, according to the *American Heritage Dictionary.*

<u>Immoderate desire for wealth; cupidity.</u>

The words *immoderate* and *cupidity* mean the following.

immoderate
Exceeding normal or appropriate bounds; extreme: immoderate spending; immoderate laughter.

See Synonyms at <u>EXCESSIVE</u> cupidity
<u>Excessive desire, especially for wealth;</u> covetousness or avarice.

It is noted that avarice has a <u>deified</u> after the word. This means money becomes their god. We refer to a deity, when we deify our wealthy and make it more important than God himself, such as Satan did. This is not to refer to all people of wealth as Kenites, but it is through ill gain and not getting money honestly that can put people in this category. A good example of what Christians did with their wealth is stated in Acts.

Acts 4:33-37

33. And with great power gave the apostles witness of the resurrection of the Lord Jesus: and great grace was upon them all.

34. Neither was there any among them that <u>lacked: for as many as were possessors of lands or houses sold them, and brought the prices of the things that were sold.</u>

35. <u>And laid them down at the apostles' feet: and distribution was made unto every man according as he had need.</u>

36. And Joses, who by the apostles was surnamed Barnabas, (which is, being interpreted, The son of consolation,) a Levite, and of the country of Cyprus,

37. <u>Having land, sold it, and brought the money,</u> and laid it at the apostles' feet. (KJV)

We are not suggesting that you sell your house and all your possessions and give them to your pastor or church, but that we should help the poor and needy in their time of distress. Use what you have to help those not as fortunate as yourself. This is a commandment from God, to "love your neighbor as yourself."

The East India Company

Remembering that *traffic* in Ezekiel meant merchants and travel for trading, thus we will see the real aim of the East India Companies. This was formed by an elite group of eight companies to control the riches of this world. <u>So pure greed is the essence of most of the secret societies of this world.</u> How do you then justify taking away other human beings' property, even killing them to get their resources and also putting the rest in slavery? The answer was very simple. You could promote the idea that these people are less than human, while through your greed you take away their possessions. All the while even though you are raping these people of their possessions, you send in missionaries to save these so- called heathen, making your side look like a savior trying to make life better. Though you did it with wrong intentions, your accomplishments would look good to others like yourself.

Thus the Kenites or Satan's offspring, in connection with the East India Companies, began to pillage and plunder what we now know as Third World countries, of their land and natural resources. There is a Latin phraseology that has been used by some of these organizations, which in English means "order out of chaos." Now the Kenites, by making those of God's Creation appear to be backwards and not up to their standards as human beings, have an excuse to produce slavery and destitution of these countries.

Although some human rights have been achieved in certain areas, it is still popular to look at others as not as good as we are. God created all souls and saw that it was good. Then what is mankind coming to; to look down on others because of a difference in color, language, or culture differences.

This was not God's plan in the beginning nor is it now. It was the Kenite scribes who in their translation of God's Word left us the impression that there was chaos first when, in fact, God created order first. When Satan was found with greed and sin in his heart, chaos came into being. This is why in verse 2 of Genesis we see the earth was without form and void, but not heaven, the abode of God. This is why God divided the dark from the light so through our Lord Jesus Christ we can keep the confusion from spreading to those who keep their faith in the true God. This is why we have chaos in this world today.

It is not God who causes this, but Satan, through his offspring, the Kenites, who virtually control all the governments of the world today. They use wars to spread confusion and division. To document what we have just said, we will go to Ezekiel and see what the Word of God has to say on this subject.

Ezek. 22:25-29

25. <u>There is a conspiracy</u> of her prophets in the midst thereof, like a <u>roaring lion</u> rav-

ening the prey; they have <u>devoured souls;</u> they have <u>taken the treasure</u> and <u>precious things;</u> they have made her <u>many widows</u> in the midst thereof.

26. <u>Her priests have violated my law,</u> and <u>have profaned mine holy things:</u> they have put <u>no difference between the holy and profane,</u> neither have they shewed <u>difference between the unclean and the clean,</u> and have <u>hid their eyes from my sabbaths,</u> and I <u>am profaned among them.</u>

27. Her princes in the midst thereof are like <u>wolves ravening the prey,</u> to <u>shed blood,</u> and to <u>destroy souls,</u> to <u>get dishonest gain.</u> 28—And her prophets have daubed them with untempered mortar, seeing vanity, and divining lies unto them, saying, <u>Thus saith the Lord GOD, when the LORD hath not spoken.</u>

28. The people of the land that <u>used oppression,</u> and <u>exercised robbery,</u> and have <u>vexed the poor and needy;</u> yea, they have <u>oppressed the stranger wrongfully.</u> (KJV)

For those who don't believe that there is a <u>conspiracy to control our world governments,</u> look at verse 25 where God said there is a conspiracy. To further show that unjust people have used the name of God to justify their indifference to different people, we read in John the words of Jesus.

John 16:2-3

2. They shall put you out of the synagogues: yea, the time cometh, that <u>whosoever</u>

killeth you will think that he doeth God service.

3. And these things will they do unto you, because they have not known the Father, nor me. (KJV)

It is noted that any religion or sect that ordains murder of other people because of color or beliefs are Kenites. It may be noted that the Nazis persecuted the Jews in the name of God. This practice is still going on today.

So we see that Christ foresaw these things happening and further we know that he told the Kenites that they were not of God, as stated in verse 3. Therefore it is not biblical to hate or look down on other people just because they are not like you.

End-Time Prophecies: First Seal

To further this thought of trading to destroy those nations that the New World Order people want to desolate in order to bring in their one-world government, we will look into the Book of Daniel and see what the prophet had to say about these end times and the New World Order.

Dan. 7:1-3

1. In the first year of Belshazzar king of Babylon Daniel had a dream and visions of his head upon his bed: then he wrote the dream, and told the sum of the matters.

2. Daniel spake and said, I saw in my vision by night, and, behold, the four winds of

the the heaven strove upon the great sea.

3.   And four great beasts came up from the sea, diverse one from another. (KJV)

This is an astounding chapter, that Daniel in his dream could write down and sum up all his dreams that he had, during his time in Babylon. Contrary to what most biblical scholars believe, this chapter is not concerned with the different empires of Babylon, Medo- Persia, the Grecian and Roman empires. To validate that this is end-time prophecy, look at verses 2 and 3 and we will show how end- time verses tie into these verses.

Matt. 24:31

31.   And he shall send his angels with a great sound of trumpet, and they shall gather together his elect from the four winds, from one end of heaven to the other. (KJV)

This is after "the great tribulation," when Christ comes for his elect and gathers them from the four corners of the earth. This then correlates with the above verse as being end times, which speak of the same four winds. To further document this end- time prophecy, we will go to verse 3 and compare it with Revelation.

Rev. 6:1

1 And I saw when the Lamb opened one of the seals, and I heard, as it were the noise of thunder, one of the four beasts saying, Come and see. (KJV)

In our studies of Daniel and Revelation, the authors have found that the animals represent different people and governments, to illustrate what God is trying to convey to us. This is also why you cannot take all the Bible literally, as it uses symbolism in a lot of its writings. So having this in mind, let's move on in Daniel and look at the rest of his prophecy.

Dan. 7

4. The first was like a lion, and had <u>eagle's wings:</u> I beheld till the <u>wings thereof were plucked,</u> and it was lifted up from the earth, and <u>made stand upon the feet as a man,</u> and a man's heart was given to it. (KJV)

The lion in Daniel's dream is Satan. To document this, here are a couple of verses from the Old and New Testament.

Ezek. 22:25

25. There is a <u>conspiracy</u> of her <u>prophets</u> in the <u>midst thereof,</u> like a <u>roaring lion</u> ravening the prey; they <u>have devoured souls;</u> they <u>have taken the treasure and precious things; they have made her many widows in the midst</u> thereof. (KJV)

1 Pet. 5:8

8. Be sober, be vigilant; because your adversary the <u>devil, as a roaring lion,</u> walketh about, seeking whom he may devour: (KJV)

In reference to Ezekiel 22:25, we request that the reader go back to what was written earlier in this chapter on the East India Companies. Going further into verse 4, we see that the lion had eagle's wings. What are these wings? When Satan was first created, he was perfect in all his ways, the anointed cherub of God. It then stands to reason that the wings are symbolic of his authority and power as were the wings on the cherub that were on the ark of the covenant, which covered the mercy seat. So how did he lose his wings or his power?

Matt. 4:1

1.   Then was Jesus led up of the Spirit into the wilderness to be <u>tempted of the devil.</u> (KJV)

Going further we read:

Matt. 4:7-11

7.   Jesus said unto him, It is written again, Thou shalt <u>not tempt the Lord thy God.</u>

8.   Again, the devil taketh him up into an exceeding high mountain, and sheweth him all the kingdoms of the world, and the glory of them;

9.   And saith unto him. All these things will I give thee, <u>if thou wilt fall down and worship me.</u>

10.   Then saith Jesus unto him, Get thee <u>hence,</u> Satan: for it is written, Thou shalt worship the Lord thy God, and him only shalt thou serve.

11.   Then the devil <u>leaveth</u> him, and, behold, angels came and ministered unto him. (KJV)

Here we see that Satan did have control over the earth at this time, because Christ did not deny the fact that he could offer him all the kingdoms of this world. But the text is very clear in verse 1 that Jesus was being tempted. Therefore when Jesus states in verse 7 not to tempt the Lord thy God, he was speaking of himself, and verse 10 that God was the only one to be worshipped. But our Lord did rebuke him and said, to get thee hence. Let's look at this word *hence.*

5217 hupago (hoop-ag'-o);
from 5259 and 71; to lead (oneself) under, i.e., withdraw or retire (as if sinking out of sight), literally or figuratively:

Also we will look at the word *leaveth.*

863 aphiemi (af-ee'-ay-mee);
from 575 and hiemi (to send; an intensive form of eimi, to go); to send forth, in various applications (as follow):

This demonstrates that Christ was in control and Satan had to withdraw under his control. Satan then lost his power on earth and was under Christ, who took him back with him when he went up to heaven, where he still is under Michael's control until Michael casts him out of heaven when his time comes before the end (Rev. 12:7- 9). Satan's departure from this earth to heaven, leads us to what our Lord Jesus Christ meant when he said to Peter:

Matt. 16:15-19

15. He saith unto them, But whom say ye that I am?

16. And Simon Peter answered and said, Thou art the Christ, the Son of the living God.

17. And Jesus answered and said unto him, Blessed art thou, Simon Barjona: for flesh

and blood bath not revealed it unto thee, but my Father which is in heaven.

18. And I say also unto thee, That thou art Peter, and upon this rock I will build my church; and the gates of hell shall not prevail it.

19. And I will give unto thee the keys of the kingdom of heaven: and whatsoever thou shalt bind on earth shall be bound in heaven: and whatsoever thou shalt loose on earth shall be loosed in heaven. (KJV)

What does this have to do with Satan's leaving? Christ asked the question, "Whom say ye that I am?" Peter answered that he was the Messiah. Christ then told him that only the Father in heaven could reveal this to him. Christ called him Peter, which means rock, which has the following meaning in the Greek:

4074 Petros (pet'-ros);
apparently a primary word; a (piece of) rock (larger than 3037); as a name, Petrus, an apostle:

This then was a small stone or a piece of the rock. Christ called him a rock because of his faith and steadfastness in his confession of Christ being the Messiah. Now here is where the Kenites or scribes created confusion, when they failed to Capitalize the real Rock, which is Christ.

4073 petra (pet'-ra); feminine of the same as 4074; a (mass of) rock (literally or figuratively):

What a difference in meanings, from a small rock to a mass of rock. As Christ is the foundation of the church, he is our rock and refuge. The keys to the kingdom of heaven is a figure of speech, meaning that Peter, along with the body of Christ, now had access to heaven because Jesus had overpowered the prince of this earth and would take him back when he ascended into heaven. When Christ did take Satan back with him, this created a vacuum, which was to be filled by the church through the Holy Spirit, who was the Comforter to come. This is why Jesus could tell Peter that whatsoever you bind on earth, he will bind in heaven. By the church having the power over all evil forces on this earth, it would be bound in heaven because the Devil is in heaven bound by Michael.

So in Daniel when it says that the lion loses his wings, it simply meant that Satan was unopposed on this earth until Christ told him to get thee hence, giving the earth's power to Christ himself who in return gave it to his body that through him we can bind the forces of evil that would hinder our walk with our Lord. This does not preclude the fact that when Satan is cast back here on earth, he will overcome the saints as he will for a short season, and regain control of this earth as written in Revelation, to fulfill prophecy.

Rev. 13:7

7.   And it was given unto him to <u>make war with the saints,</u> and to <u>overcome them:</u> and <u>power was given him over all kindreds, and tongues, and nations</u>. (KJV)

Going further into **Satan being the Lion**, we will turn to Revelation again.

Rev. 6:2

2. And I saw, and behold a <u>white horse:</u> and he that <u>sat on him had a bow;</u> and a <u>crown</u> was given unto him: and he went forth conquering, and to conquer. (KJV)

This does not mention the word **lion,** but if we look at who is on the white horse and what he is carrying, we will get a little different point of view.

5115 toxon (tox'-on);
from the *base of 5088;* a bow <u>(apparently as the simplest fabric):</u>

Very interesting that simplest of fabric is used. This does not seem like a bow that shoots arrows. Going into the root of this word will give us a little insight into how Satan can pollute this world when he comes back to earth.

5088 tikto (tik'-to);
a strengthened form of a primary teko (tek'- o) (which is used only as alternate in certain tenses); <u>to produce from seed, as a mother, a plant, the earth, etc.),</u> literally or figuratively: KJV—bear, be born, <u>bring forth, be </u>delivered, be in travail

Looking at the first definition of *bow,* it has an interesting meaning that is not what most literal readers think of as a bow. No arrows are mentioned, and here we have a fabric. Breaking down the definition of bow to its prime, we see seed from a mother. This seed is children. This weaves a definite message into this story that Satan's seed, the Kenites, have woven into history their plan to control the earth. Christ also comes on a white horse spoken of in Revelation 19:11, which is the true Christ.

Rev. 19:11

11. And I saw heaven opened, and behold a <u>white horse;</u> and he that sat upon him was <u>called Faithful and True,</u> and in righteousness he doth judge and make war. (KJV)

Satan, running true to form, will try to duplicate his return, hoping to make believers think he is Messiah. Having an adversary that is so devious and crafty, with his children following in his footsteps, don't you think that all these so-called wars and rumors of wars could be contrived to keep the nations and the people divided as it is true in the following statement: "United we stand but divided we fall." Jesus had this to say about the end times and wars.

Matt. 24:6-7

6. And ye shall hear of wars and <u>rumors</u> of wars: see that ye be not troubled: for all these things must come to pass, <u>but the end is not yet.</u>

7. For nation shall rise against nation, and kingdom against kingdom: and there shall be famines, and pestilences, and earthquakes, in divers places. (KJV)

The word *rumor* has the following meaning.

189 akoe (ak-o-ay');
from 191; <u>hearing (the act, the sense or the thing heard):</u>

Doesn't this ring a bell? Is this what you hear in the news concerning the Third World countries and Bosnia? This period now has to be in the end times, that Christ was speaking about because, until the atomic bomb, the rumor of the world's destruction in a matter of hours could not have existed.

Since World War II, there has not been any power that could match the United States, especially with the invention of the atom bomb. Knowing this, the so- called world leaders whom we feel take their orders from the High Cabal, who are really in control, have to ferment trouble spots to keep the tension going. A good example was in Orwell's *1984.*

During the bombing of London and Rotterdam, it is recorded that Sir Winston Churchill, Prime Minister of England, was quoted as saying, "The bombardment of London, the bombardment of Rotterdam, and the total war at sea, the High Cabal must be at work." Buckminister Fuller also acknowledged the High Cabal, whom he also called the Super Elite. The fact is that these super secret organizations need an enemy to fight, so they can always find a way to tax you and me to pay for these so- called wars.

At the end of World War II, this organization needed another enemy to hate so they would have an excuse to plunder our resources in taxes and manpower. This is why the Russians were the only ones to go into Berlin first at the end of the war, and why at Yalta the Big Four divided up Europe, and Russia was allowed to create an Eastern Bloc. There is a Latin saying that fits right into this philosophy that seems to be appropriate to give the readers, and what we feel is the thinking of this organization. "ODERINT DUM METUANT," which means "LET THEM HATE, SO

So after World War II, in order to keep the pressure on the public at large, they created what was called a "Cold War." We have just one question: what is cold about war? Anyone who has ever been in a war knows that it is not cold. This is just what the world needed after a tremendous struggle during World War II. This so-called Cold War was also a <u>farce.</u> So under the alleged threat to national security, the government could take away your liberties, suspend parts or all of the Constitution. This is happening in America, today, with crime on the rampage and drugs being one of the top categories of crime.

Our illustrious leaders will use these issues to take away your liberties in the guise of fighting crime and drugs. They have also followed the East India Companies' policy of referring to people other than themselves as not human.

A good example is the book *The Bell Curve,* which they say shows that some groups do not have the same mental activity as others. If you do not believe this, then read the book on this subject. We help this along with so-called jokes depicting different groups in our country. Through the media, and a lot of rhetoric, the color of a person is used to make each of us distrust each other and divide us so we can be controlled. The authors believe that the O. J. Simpson trial was a good example. When he could not be framed for the crime, the media used it to divide the different nationalities. Just look at the polls taken on this subject to see how the division between guilt or innocence is split between the different groups.

The Second Seal

Looking now into Daniel, we will further illustrate that God through Daniel related that this was going to happen. We will look at the next part of Daniel, chapter 7.

Dan. 7:5

5.   And behold another beast, a second, like to a <u>bear,</u> and it raised up itself on one side, and it had three ribs in the mouth of it between the teeth of it: and they said thus unto it, Arise, devour much flesh. (KJV)

Just what does the bear in Daniel have to do with the end times? Let us look at its meaning and see just what it represents.

1677 dob (dobe);
or (fully) dowb (dobe); from 1680; <u>the bear (as slow):</u>

Most readers knows that Russia and China are referred to as a bear; however we feel that what Daniel is really referring to is the fact that this bear, in its meaning as slow, is very significant. If you break down this meaning, it also means sluggish. Who has been slower in meeting the growing standard of living than the Third World countries, like Africa, South America, China, etc. These have been the prime targets of what is left of the East India Companies and the High Cabal, in order to keep those non-industrialized nations under control.

Using the GATT trade agreement along with NAFTA, the world organization can control all countries. In 2 Peter we can read about these agreements affecting our trade and its use by Satan.

2 Pet. 2:3

3. And through <u>covetousness</u> shall they with <u>feigned</u> words <u>make merchandise</u> of you: whose judgment now of a long time lingereth not, and their damnation slumbereth not. (KJV)

Looking at the meanings of the underlined words, we will get a clearer picture of what Peter saw.

4124 pleonexia (pleh-on-ex-ee'-ah);
from 4123; <u>avarice, i.e., (by implication) fraudulency, extortion:</u>
KJV—covetous<u>(- ness) practices, greediness.</u>

This word *covetousness* matches what the new trade agreements were set up for. Through fraud and extortion, these agreements will make each country, including our own, bow down under the rule of the New World Order. In the agreements signed, each country can be extorted into complying by not excluding their goods from trade until they conform to what the so-called bodies of the agreement want them to do. It is only for greed and Satan's control of the wealth of this world that these agreements were put into operation.

Look at the **word** *feigned.* This is another example of how the scribes of the Kenites misused a word.

4112 plastos (plas-tos');
from 4111; moulded, i.e., (by implication) artificial or (figuratively) fictitious (false):

The meanings "moulded" or "artificial" and
"fictitious" are important when you go into the
prime root of the word *plasso.*

4111 plasso (plas'-so);
a primary verb; to mould, i.e., shape or fabricate:

To shape or fabricate is exactly what is spoken of in Revelation 6:2 in which we learned that
the word *bow* means fabric or molding. In addition, it also meant from his seed putting the
Kenites in control of all the governments of this
world. Continuing in Peter we see that to make
merchandise has this meaning in the Greek.

1710 emporeuomai (em-por-yoo'-om-ahee);
from 1722 and 4198; to travel in (a country as
a peddler), i.e., (by implication) to trade:
KJV—buy and sell, make merchandise.

To make merchandise, this is nothing more
than using these trade agreements in other
countries, illustrating the meaning "to travel in a
country." Using these different trade agreements
has caused what we know as downsizing in
companies. It is also a tool to circumvent the labor unions to achieve their goal of world domi-
nance.

To quote a phrase from Franklin D. Roose-
velt, "Nothing happens in politics by accident,
but it is planned that way." Sometimes when we
see things happening in government that may

seem dumb, those causing them know exactly what they are doing.

The bear raised up on one side indicates the use of puppet leaders to keep each country in check. It is interesting to note that bears do not eat ribs or bones, so starvation is a method that is used to keep these countries under control. Devouring much flesh is pretty much self-explanatory, as we know what the communist regimes have done to the world, in the matter of lost lives. To tie in Revelation with Daniel, we will show that the red horse is the same as the bear.

Rev. 6:4

4.   And there went out another horse that was red: and power was given to him and sat thereon to <u>take peace from the earth,</u> and that <u>they should kill one another:</u> and <u>there was given unto him a great sword</u>. (KJV)

Who then gives the orders feeding this mechanism that destroys lives and property? You guessed it if you said the High Cabal. The Kenites are now paving the way for the Beast of Revelation, which is a one-world government. It will come as prophesied, but as Christians we can be ready, by using God's Word, and faith in him that saved us. Isaiah had this to say about these times:

Isa. 13:5-8

5.   They come from a far country, from the end of heaven, even the LORD, and the weapons of his indignation, to <u>destroy</u> the

whole land.

6. Howl ye; for the <u>day of the LORD is at hand;</u> it shall come as a destruction from the Almighty.

7. Therefore shall all hands be faint, and every man's heart shall melt:

8. And they shall be afraid: pangs and <u>sorrows</u> shall take hold of them; they shall be in pain as a woman that travaileth: they shall be amazed one at another; their faces shall be as flames. (KJV)

The word *destroy* in verse 5 has the following meaning.

2254 chabal (khaw-bal');
a primitive root; to <u>wind tightly</u> (as a rope), i.e., to bind; specifically, by a <u>pledge;</u> figuratively, to <u>pervert, destroy;</u> also to writhe in pain (especially of parturition):

The word *sorrows* in verse 8 have this meaning in the Hebrew:

2256 chebel (kheh'-bel);
or chebel (khay'- bel); from 2254; a rope <u>(as twisted),</u> especially a measuring line; by implication, a district or inheritance (as measured); or a noose (as of cords); figuratively, <u>a company (as if tied together);</u> also a throe (especially of parturition); also ruin:

Can you see that the meanings are so similar and also the words *chabel* and *chebel* are so close to *Cabal* that even in Isaiah's time our Father prophesied this High Cabal and the birth of the New World Order. But the good news is that he will destroy it with the brightness of his coming.

The Third Seal

Going back into chapter 7 of Daniel and continuing on, we read the following.

Dan. 7:6

6. After this I beheld, and to another, like a <u>leopard,</u> which had upon the back of it <u>four wings of a fowl;</u> the <u>beast had also four heads;</u> and <u>dominion was given to it.</u> (KJV)

As we know a leopard does not change his spots. The apostle Paul said in Ephesians that the Lord wanted a church without spot or wrinkle. These spots are the Kenites, the offspring of Satan. Also, *wrinkle* has this meaning.

Informal. <u>A clever trick, method, or device, especially one that is new and different; an innovation.</u>

Christ does not want new innovative ideas about his Word. He wants us to stick to his teachings and not waver from the truth. Daniel saw in verse 6 how these leopards or Kenites in the end times will control the four powers of the earth. This is the essence of all government entities: Political, religious, educational, and monetary. Looking at the meaning of *fowl,* you can get a better understanding of what we mean.

5775 'owph (ofe);
from 5774; a bird (as covered with feathers, or rather as <u>covering with wings),</u> often collectively:

Looking at the prime of this word makes it a little clearer.

5774 'uwph (oof);
a primitive root; to <u>cover (with wings or obscurity);</u> hence (as denominative from 5775) <u>to fly;</u> also (by implication of dimness) faint (from the darkness of swooning):

These meanings unfold to us a picture of the High Cabal, which uses the different wings of government with obscurity, not giving the people at large any hint of how they control the different governments. To further document what we are saying; let us go to Revelation 6.

Rev. 6:5-6

5.   And when he had opened the <u>third seal.</u> I heard the third beast say, Come and see. And I beheld, and lo a black horse; <u>and he that sat on him had a pair of balances in his hand.</u>

6.   And I heard a voice in the midst of the four beasts say, A <u>measure of wheat for a penny, and three measures of barley for a penny;</u> and see thou hurt not the oil and the wine. (KJV)

We see false balances being used to keep the poor still poorer and elevate the rich through inflation. Money that is used by the Federal Reserve Board, not backed by a common source, such as gold or silver. False agencies in government prevent the economic recovery of any nation to its full capacity. The prophet Amos also saw the end times and these terrible times in which we are living now.

Amos 8:1-6

1. Thus hath the Lord GOD shewed unto me: and behold a <u>basket of summer fruit.</u>

2. And he said, Amos, what seest thou? And I said, A basket of summer fruit. Then said the LORD unto me, <u>The end is come upon my people of Israel; I will not again pass by them any more.</u>

3. And the songs of the temple shall be howlings in that day, saith the Lord GOD; there shall be many <u>dead bodies</u> in every place; they shall cast them forth with silence.

4. Hear this, 0 ye that swallow up the needy, <u>even to make the poor of the land to fail,</u>

5. Saying, When will the new moon be gone, <u>that we may sell corn? and the sabbath, that we may set forth wheat, making the ephah small, and the shekel great, and falsifying the balances by deceit?</u>

6. <u>That we may buy the poor for silver, and the needy for a pair of shoes; yea, and sell the refuse of the wheat?</u> (KJV)

This is not only end- time prophecy, but it is actually happening to us now. The true Messiah comes in at a harvest time and in verse 2. Our Lord says he will not pass by anymore. The dead bodies are symbolic of the lost souls swallowed up by Satan as the false messiah. Going further in the Book of Amos, we will see what the real famine in the end times will be.

Amos 8:11

11. Behold, the days come, said the Lord GOD, that <u>I will send a famine in the land, not a famine of bread,</u> nor a <u>thirst for water,</u> but of <u>hearing the words of the LORD:</u> (KJV)

We know that the Word is not being taught correctly in these end times. The Word has been perverted and God's people are in a famine for the hearing of the true Word of God. This also coincides with Amos and the dead bodies.

Matt. 10:28

28. And fear not them which kill the body, but are not able to kill the soul: but rather fear him which is able to <u>destroy both soul and body in hell</u>. (KJV)

The Fourth Seal

The **last beast** of Daniel reads as follows:

Dan. 7:7-8

7. After this I saw in the night visions, and behold a fourth beast, dreadful and terrible, and strong exceedingly; and it had great iron teeth: it devoured and brake in pieces, and stamped the residue with the feet of it: and it was diverse from <u>all the beasts</u> that were before it; and it had <u>ten horns.</u>

8. I considered the horns, and behold, there came up among them <u>another little horn,</u> before whom there were three of the first horns plucked up by the roots: and, behold, in this horn were eyes like the eyes of man, and a mouth speaking great

things. (KJV)

This shows that the fourth beast of Daniel is the same as the fourth seal of Revelation, which is the Little Horn of Daniel, who is Satan or death.

Rev. 6:7-8

7.   And when he had opened the <u>fourth seal,</u> I heard the voice of the fourth beast say, Come and see.

8.   And I looked, and behold a pale horse: and <u>his name that sat on him was Death,</u> and Hell followed with him. And power was given unto them over the fourth part of the earth, to kill with sword, and with hunger, and with death, and with the beasts of the earth. (KJV)

To conclude this chapter and the correlation between the fourth beast of Daniel and those of Revelation, we see that verses 7 and 8 correspond to the ten- horned beast of Revelation.

Rev. 13:1-7

1.   And I stood upon the sand of the sea, and saw a beast rise up out of the sea, having seven heads and <u>ten horns,</u> and upon his horns ten crowns, and upon his heads the name of blasphemy.

2.   And the beast which I saw was like unto a <u>leopard,</u> and his feet were as the feet of a <u>bear,</u> and his mouth as the mouth of a <u>li-on:</u> and the dragon gave him his power, and his seat, and great authority.

3.   And I saw one of his heads as it were

wounded to death; and his deadly wound was healed: and all the world wondered after the beast.

4. And they worshipped the dragon which gave power unto the beast: and they worshipped the beast, saying, Who is like unto the beast? who is able to make war with him?

5. And there was given unto him a mouth speaking great things and blasphemies; and power was given unto him to continue forty and two months.

6. And he opened his mouth in blasphemy against God, to blaspheme his name, and his tabernacle, and them that dwell in heaven.

7. And it was given unto him to <u>make war with the saints,</u> and to <u>overcome them:</u> and power was given him over all kindreds, and tongues, and nations. (KJV)

What we have revealed is how the Kenites, Satan's seed, are setting up their one- world system, using deception and the world government to bring into existence a system that Satan himself will use when he comes on the scene as the false messiah. It is our hope that the children of God will understand that they have to be into the Word to prepare themselves for these end times.

The next chapter will deal with the Great Tribulation and the churches.

6
The Deity of Christ, the Church, and the Great Tribulation

We will show in this chapter and in chapter 9, that the Church or the Body of Christ will be here during the Great Tribulation. Why are we so sure that this will happen? Let us lay a little background on the subject. The church has been steeped in tradition, which has led us from the thorough examination of God's Word, thereby allowing traditions to be taught without any challenge or questioning of what are sometimes contradictory or unclear concepts. This was a big mistake in Paul's time, for he addressed the Church at Corinth with this admonition:

1 Cor. 10:1-6

1. Moreover, brethren, <u>I would not that ye should be ignorant,</u> how that all our fathers were under the cloud, and all passed through the sea;

2. And were all baptized unto Moses in the cloud and in the sea;

3. And did all <u>eat the same spiritual meat;</u>

4. And did all <u>drink same spiritual drink:</u> for they drank of that <u>spiritual Rock</u> that followed them: and that <u>Rock was Christ.</u>

5. But with many of them God was not well pleased: for they were overthrown in the <u>wilderness.</u>

6. Now these things were <u>our examples,</u> to the intent we should not lust after evil things, as they also lusted. (KJV)

Who Is or Was Jesus Christ? Was He God in the Flesh?

Yes! He was God in the flesh. Who was he before he was incarnated into the flesh on this earth? It is a common traditional belief that Christ (the Word) has always been God's Son. In this context it would make you believe that God had a wife and produced a son. As you may recall, in chapter 2 of this book, we established that Christ was the Word, which created all things. To show that Christ was in <u>the state of being God,</u> let's read what Paul had to say about Christ in Colossians

Col. 2:9

9. For in him dwelleth all the <u>fulness of the Godhead bodily.</u> (KJV)

Looking at the meaning of **Godhead**, we have this meaning, according to *Thayer's:*

2320 theotes-deity,
the state<u> of being God,</u> Godhead

So Christ was not a son in his prehuman state, but was God (the Word) placed in human flesh. We will reinforce this statement with the following verses:

John 1:1

1. In the beginning was the <u>Word,</u> and the <u>Word</u> was with God, and <u>the Word was God</u>. (KJV)

To take a position that Christ was a god or a lesser god than the Father, would be thoroughly contradictory to the following Scriptures as well as the verses quoted above:

John 4:24

24. <u>God is a Spirit:</u> and they that worship him must <u>worship him in spirit and in truth</u>. (KJV)

John 5:16-18

16. And therefore did the Jews persecute Jesus, and sought to slay him, because he had done these things on the sabbath day.

17. But Jesus answered them, <u>My Father worketh hitherto, and I work.</u>

18. Therefore the Jews sought the more to kill him, because he not only had broken the sabbath, <u>but said also that God was his Father, making himself equal with God.</u> (KJV)

The Jews in this case are clearly the Kenites, who were trying to kill him. In John 5:18, it is very clear that Jesus declared that he was equal with God and not less than God in his flesh form. Continuing in this context, he explains the consequences of rejecting him.

John 5:22-23

22. For the Father judgeth no man, but hath

committed all judgment unto the Son:

23. That all men <u>should honour the Son, even as they honour the Father. He that honoureth not the Son honoureth not the Father which hath sent him</u>. (KJV)

John 5:39

39. <u>Search the scriptures;</u> for in them ye think ye have eternal life: and they are they <u>which testify of me</u>. (KJV)

Jesus makes it clear that all Scriptures were pertaining to him, which is further substantiated in John.

John 14:6-9

6. Jesus saith unto him, <u>I am the way, the truth, and the life: no man cometh unto the Father, but by me.</u>

7. If ye <u>had known me, ye should have known my Father also:</u> and from <u>henceforth ye know him, and have seen him.</u>

8. <u>Philip saith unto him, Lord, shew us the Father,</u> and it sufficeth us.

9. Jesus saith unto him, <u>Have I been so long time with you, and yet hast thou not known me,</u> Philip? <u>he that hath seen me hath seen the Father;</u> and how sayest thou then, Shew us the Father? (KJV)

John 17:4-5

4. I have glorified thee on the earth: I have finished the work which thou gayest me to do.

5. <u>And now, O Father, glorify thou me with thine own self</u> with the glory which I had

with thee <u>before the world was</u>. (KJV)

In the above Scriptures, which seem to be self- explanatory, Jesus makes it clear to Philip just who he was in John 17:5. Jesus asks the Father to glorify him back into the glory that he held before the world was, which was universal worship with God. And to substantiate this, we go further into this chapter of John.

John 17:17-19

17. Sanctify them through thy truth: <u>thy word is truth.</u>

18. As thou hast sent me into the world, even so have I also sent them into the world.

19. And for their sakes <u>I sanctify myself,</u> that they also might be sanctified through the truth. (KJV)

The last verse declares that he is God. When Christ can sanctify himself, then this puts him in an interchangeable state with the Father. Giving the reader further proof of Christ being God, we go back into the Book of John.

John 20:27-28

27. Then saith he to Thomas, Reach hither thy finger, and behold my hands; and reach hither thy hand, and thrust it into my side: and be not faithless, but believing.

28. And Thomas answered and said unto him, <u>My Lord and my God</u>. (KJV)

Here Thomas not only declares him as his Lord, he also confesses that he is God. When Thomas realized that Jesus, whom he knew had died, was now raised from the dead, he then understood that Christ was the ultimate sacrifice mentioned in Psalms 40 verse 5.

Ps. 40:5-7

5. Many, <u>O LORD my God,</u> are thy wonderful works which thou hast done, and thy thoughts which are to us- ward: they cannot be reckoned up in order unto thee: if I would declare and speak of them, they are more than can be numbered.

6. Sacrifice and offering thou didst not desire; mine ears hast thou opened: burnt offering and sin offering hast thou not required.

7. <u>Then said I, Lo, I come: in the volume of the book it is written of me</u>, (KJV)

To further strengthen that Christ was our sacrifice proving that he was God, we will go to Hebrews.

Heb. 10:4-7

4. <u>For it is not possible that the blood of bulls and of goats should take away sins.</u>

5. <u>Wherefore when he cometh into the world, he saith, Sacrifice and offering thou wouldest not, but a body bast thou prepared me:</u>

6. In burnt offerings and sacrifices for sin thou hast had no pleasure.

7. <u>Then said I, Lo, I come (in the volume of the book it is written of me.) to do thy will, O God</u>. (KJV)

<u>To continue in our documentation that</u>

<u>Christ is God, we read in Matthew this account of his Godhead.</u>

Matt. 4:1

1. <u>Then was Jesus</u> led up of the <u>Spirit</u> into the wilderness <u>to be tempted of the devil</u>. (KJV)

The statement made in Matthew is very clear that the person being tempted is Jesus only. Going further into this chapter of Matthew, the following Scriptures will clarify the point that Christ was God and the Devil should not try to tempt him.

Matt. 4:5-10

5. Then the devil taketh him up into the holy city, and setteth him on a pinnacle of the temple,

6. And saith unto him, <u>If thou be the Son of God,</u> cast thyself down: for it is written. He shall give his angels charge concerning thee: and in their hands they shall bear thee up, lest at any time thou dash thy foot against a stone.

7. Jesus said unto him, It is written again, <u>Thou shalt not tempt the Lord thy God.</u>

8. Again, the devil taketh him up into an exceeding high mountains, and sheweth him all the kingdoms of the world, and the glory of them;

9. And saith unto him, All these things will I give thee, if thou wilt fall down and worship me.

10. Then saith Jesus unto him, Get thee hence, Satan: for it is written, <u>Thou shalt worship the Lord thy God, and him only shalt thou serve</u>. (KJV)

Christ is very clear in the above verses when he told Satan that he could not tempt him; he was his God, making him coequal with the Father, and to be worshipped.

Paul's Clear Warning concerning Vain Philosophy and Tradition

As we go further into the churches and the Tribulation, Paul was very clear in the following verses about vain philosophy and traditions of men.

Col. 2:6-8

6. As ye have therefore received Christ Jesus the Lord, so walk ye in him:

7. Rooted and built up in him, and established in the faith, as ye have been taught, abounding therein with thanksgiving.

8. Beware lest <u>any man spoil</u> you through <u>philosophy</u> and <u>vain deceit,</u> after the <u>tradition of men,</u> after the <u>rudiments</u> of the world, and not after Christ. (KJV)

What Paul refers to in verse 8 is that men are spoiled, through vain philosophy, and vain deceit. They follow after the traditions of men and the rudiments of the world. We as Christians should be rooted in the word, not traditions. Therefore to see what will happen in the end times, we should look at what happened in times past.

The Babylon of Nebuchadnezzar's Times and the Babylon of End Times

The Book of Revelation in chapter 17 refers to Babylon where the great whore sits. In chapter 18 Babylon is said to be fallen. Is this the Babylon of old or is there another meaning to the Babylon of the end times? The New Testament speaks of the past as things that will happen again in the future. Paul uses this example in Colossians.

Col. 2:16-17

16. <u>Let no man therefore judge you in meat, or in drink,</u> or in respect of an holy day, or of the new moon, or of the sabbath days:

17. <u>Which are a shadow of things to come;</u> but the body is of Christ. (KJV)

Paul was saying that what happened to the children of Israel, <u>during their flight through the wilderness,</u> was just an example to us. In other words the past is to be viewed as an <u>example of things to come,</u> and to be a lesson we can learn from. In Paul's time, the only written Scripture he and the Apostles had were manuscripts of the Old Testament. During this time the New Testament was being written. This is why <u>both parts of the Bible, are equally important.</u>

Going into Scripture we can learn another example that concerns end times, and to show us what will happen to the Church, or the Body of Christ during the Great Tribulation.

Rev. 17:1-5

1. And there came one of the seven angels which had the seven vials, and talked with me, saying unto me, Come hither, I will shew unto thee the <u>judgment of the great whore</u> that sitteth upon many waters:

2. <u>With whom the kings of the earth have committed fornication, and the inhabitants of the earth have been made drunk with the wine of her fornication.</u>

3. So he carried me away in <u>the spirit into the wilderness:</u> and I saw a woman sit upon a scarlet coloured beast, full of names of blasphemy, having <u>seven heads and ten horns.</u>

4. And the woman was arrayed in purple and scarlet colour, and decked with gold and precious stones and pearls, having a golden cup in her hand full of abominations and filthiness of her fornication:

5. And upon her forehead was a name written, <u>MYSTERY BABYLON</u> THE GREAT, THE MOTHER OF HARLOTS AND ABOMINATIONS OF THE EARTH. (KJV)

We know that Babylon was defeated by the Medes and Persians, about 426 B.C. So how could Babylon be used in the end times? Let's look at the meaning of Babylon, and maybe we can see why it is used again. In the Hebrew, Babylon has the following meaning.

894 Babel (baw-bel');
from 1101; <u>confusion; Babel</u> (i.e., Babylon), including Babylonia and the Babylonian empire:

Babylon is not only a city but when used symbolically can mean Babel or confusion. This is exactly what will happen in the end times. There will be confusion. Unless the truth is known by God's people, they will be kept in confusion. The Greek definition can explain this a little more.

897 Babulon (bab-oo-lone');
of Hebrew origin [894]; Babylon, the capitol of Chaldaea (literally or figuratively [as a <u>type of tyranny</u>]):

Here we have tyranny, which is what Satan will impose, to control this earth, during his brief reign. You might say at this point, well, what has this to do with the Church? Some will say that we will not be here, so what is the point? Well, we will look further into Revelation and see just what the Scripture says about Babylon and the Church.

Rev. 18:2-4

2.   And he cried mightily with a strong voice, saying, <u>Babylon the great is fallen, is fallen,</u> and is become the habitation of devils, and the hold of every foul spirit, and a cage of every unclean and hateful bird.

3.   For all nations have drunk of the wine of the wrath of her fornication, and the kings of earth have committed fornication with her, and the merchants of the earth are waxed rich through the abundance of her

delicacies.

4. And I heard another voice from heaven, saying, <u>Come out of her, my people, that ye be not partakers of her sins, and that ye receive not of her plagues</u>. (KJV)

Verse 2 declares that Babylon has fallen. We know that in the first part of this chapter, Babylon fell approximately 426 B.C. So this is not Babylon of old, but a type of one to come in the end times. We have confusion and tyranny, which is Satan's trademark. Through this confusion Satan will come on the scene, making most people who believe he is Christ, and will gather those who know not the truth to him. This is what Jesus meant when speaking in John:

John 5:43

43. I am come in my Father's name, and ye receive me not: if <u>another shall come in his own name, him ye will receive.</u> (KJV)

This shows that people will believe that Satan is Christ; they will believe the lie of Antichrist.

What about the Church? In verse 4 we read the following: "Come out of her, my people." Who are the people the Father is talking about? His people, his body, his bride. How can you come out of something, if you are not there in the first place? The word *come* means <u>to issue</u> in *Strong's Exhaustive Concordance.* In *Thayer's,* we have the following meaning:

1831 exerchomai-

1. <u>to go or to come forth of, with mention of the place out of which one goes, or the</u>

point from which he departs

2. used of those who leave a place of their own accord

3. used of those who are expelled or cast out

So what the Scripture clearly states is, that when the time comes, the Father is going to send the plagues on Antichrist, and all who follow Christ, in his body will come out of this confusion, and tyranny, for we know the Father will protect his own.

Resisting Satan in the End Times

What makes the authors think that we should submit under Satan at all? Why not resist Satan in the beginning, and fight him with whatever weapons or resources we have at hand? This includes his one-world government also. We have shown that history does repeat itself, so we will look at the first Babylon, and what God told his people concerning the coming armies of Babylon.

Remembering what Paul said about the Old Testament being a shadow of things to come, Jeremiah was there when Jerusalem was taken captive. Did God tell them to fight off the invaders? Let's see what the prophet said.

Jer. 27:2-15

2. Thus saith the LORD to me; Make thee bonds and yokes, and put them upon thy neck.

3. And send them to the king of Edom, and

to the king of Moab, and to the king of the Ammonites, and to the king of Tyrus, and to the king of Zidon, by the hand of the messengers which come to Jerusalem unto Zedekiah king of Judah;

4. And command them to say unto their masters, Thus saith the LORD of hosts, the God of Israel; Thus shall ye say unto your masters;

5. <u>I have made the earth, the man and the beast that are upon the ground, by my great power and by my outstretched arm, and have given it unto whom it seemed meet unto me.</u>

6. And now have I given all these lands into the hand of Nebuchadnezzar the king of Babylon, my servant; and the beasts of the field have I given him also to serve him.

7. And all nations shall serve him, and his son, and his son's son, until the very time of his land come: and then many nations and great kings shall serve themselves of him.

8. And it shall come to pass, <u>that the nation and kingdom which will not serve</u> the same Nebuchadnezzar the king of <u>Baby-lon,</u> and <u>that will not put their neck under the yoke of the king of Babylon,</u> that nation <u>will I punish,</u> saith the LORD, with the sword, and with the <u>famine, and with the pestilence,</u> until I have consumed them by his hand.

9. Therefore <u>hearken not ye to your proph-</u>

ets, nor to your diviners, nor to your dreamers, nor to your enchanters, nor to your sorcerers, which speak unto you, saying, Ye shall not serve the king of Babylon:

10. For they prophesy a lie unto you, to remove you far from your land; and that I should drive you out, and ye should perish.

11. But the nations that bring their neck under the yoke of the king of Babylon, and serve him, those will I let remain still in their own land, saith the LORD; and they shall till it, and dwell therein.

12. I spake also to Zedekiah king of Judah according to all these words, saying, Bring your necks under the yoke of the king of Babylon, and serve him and his people, and live.

13. Why will ye die, thou and thy people, by the sword, by the famine, and by the pestilence, as the LORD hath spoken against the nation that will not serve the king of Babylon?

14. Therefore hearken not unto the words of the prophets that speak unto you, saying, Ye shall not serve the king of Babylon: for they prophesy a lie unto you.

15. For I have not sent them, saith the LORD, yet they prophesy a lie in my name; that I might drive you out, and that ye might perish, ye, and the prophets that prophesy unto you.

This is an astounding revelation in Scripture pertaining to Babylon and what we should do in the end times. Did God say fight them at all costs? Not hardly. What he said was to submit under his yoke. This may be hard to believe, but this is what Scripture says. Well, you might say, that was in the Old Testament, and does not concern us now. Dear readers, this again is a shadow of things to come. If Babylon or confusion exits in the end times, then God's rules still apply. As stated before, you cannot come out of something that you are not already in.

This is not a fleshly battle that we have been raging throughout history, but a spiritual war between good and evil. To put it another way, between God and Satan. All events recorded in the Bible are really God's people fighting against Satan's forces. You can put flesh and blood on those people of biblical times, as they were just like us. They had feelings, emotions of love and hate. They went through the same kinds of trials and tests, we go through. But the culmination of this Earth Age, will be when Satan is booted out of Heaven by Michael, and comes here on earth to sit up his brief kingdom, as recorded in Revelation.

Rev. 12:7-9

7. And there was war in heaven: <u>Michael and his angels fought against the dragon; and the dragon fought and his angels,</u>

8. And prevailed not; <u>neither was their place found any more in heaven.</u>

9. And the <u>great dragon was cast out, that</u>

old serpent, called the Devil, and Satan, which deceiveth the whole world: he was cast out into the earth, and his angels were cast out with him. (KJV)

In our opinion this is end- time prophecy, as we will substantiate later in this chapter, that Satan is in heaven until he is cast out.

Continuing in Jeremiah chapter 27, the children of God were warned not to resist the king of Babylon, which is a type of Satan. We must reject any teaching by the prophets or preachers that we should resist, "or there will be peace" is a lie. This earth will not have peace, nor will the church, until Christ comes to destroy evil from the earth.

Verse 9 refers to the prophets who say we will not serve the king of Babylon. We know that we will not serve Antichrist, but this is a shadow of things to come as the prophets or teachers of our day, tell us that we will not be under the yoke of Antichrist. In Jeremiah' s day, they were not to resist the armies of Babylon, but to go under their yoke. In Revelation we get the same message.

Rev. 13:8-10

8. And all that dwell upon the earth shall worship him, whose names are not written in the book of life and of the Lamb slain from the foundation of the world.

9. If any man have an ear, let him hear.

10. He that leadeth into captivity shall go into captivity: he that killeth with the sword must be killed with the sword. Here is the

<u>patience and the faith of the saints</u>. (KJV)

Verse 8 clearly shows that when Satan is on this earth, all who worship him will be those whose names are not written in the Lamb's Book of Life.

When we check out meanings of verse 10 in the manuscripts, we found that verse 10 amplifies verse 8 and our Lord puts emphasis on verse 10 when he says, "he that leadeth into captivity." The word **leadeth** has the following meaning.

4863 sunago (soon-ag'-0);
from 4862 and 71; <u>to lead together,</u> i.e., collect or convene; specifically, to entertain (hospitably):

In Thayer's definition, we find:

4863 sunago-
1.   <u>to gather together, to gather; to draw together, to collect:</u>
     a)   used of fishes
     b)   used of a net in which they are caught

To lead then is not one person, or a leader, but a group of people. It also states that if you kill by the sword, you will die by the sword. This is the same admonition that Jeremiah gave when Babylon was about to take Jerusalem. This is also a word to those who in our great country, have chosen to fight to the death rather than give in to a one-world system or government. If your faith is in Christ, then your endurance or patience will win out in his name. God is faithful to his chosen people, and will always give them a way to escape, whatever comes upon them. In 1

Corinthians we see a promise that is everlasting.

1 Cor. 10:13

13. There hath <u>no temptation</u> taken you but such as is <u>common to man:</u> but <u>God is faithful,</u> who will <u>not suffer you to be tempted above that ye are able; but will with the temptation also make a way to escape, that ye may be able to bear it</u>. (KJV)

This not only applies to your daily life, as it is now, but to the future when we have to face a great tribulation, that will be the hardest of them all. What makes the Great Tribulation so great is that God's people have not, in the past, or now, ever had to face an enemy so powerful as Satan himself. Being that he is the master of deception, and will be so convincing that he is Christ, even the elect would not be saved, except that God had shortened the days of his reign on earth (Mark 13:20).

You may say to all of this that we are talking about end times, and the Old Testament has nothing to do with what is happening now. Well, the Old Testament is for our knowledge of things that happened before, and will happen again. As it is written:

Eccles. 1:9

9. <u>The thing that hath been, it is that which shall be; and that which is done is that which shall be done: and there is no new thing under the sun</u>. (KJV)

They did not have a New Testament written during Christ's time, or even Paul's. They relied on the old Scriptures, to guide them into what was happening then, and the future. So Babylon of old, and the future, will be played out on the stage of this world, and all the rules apply now as did then, and so it will be when Antichrist comes on the scene. We will be taken into captivity, but not in our minds, for we will have the seal of God <u>in</u> our foreheads, or to put it plainly, the truth <u>in</u> our minds.

The Church and the Great Tribulation

To further prove that the church will be here during the Great Tribulation, we will go into the parable that our Lord taught about the tares. Here Jesus tells an explicit story that spans from creation to the end of time.

Matt. 13:24-30

24. Another parable put he forth unto them, saying, The kingdom of heaven is likened unto a man which sowed good seed in his field:

25. But while men slept, <u>his enemy came and sowed tares among the wheat,</u> and went his way.

26. But when the blade was sprung up, and brought forth fruit, then appeared the tares also.

27. So the servants of the householder came and said unto him, Sir, didst not thou sow good seed in thy field? from whence then hath it tares?

28. He said unto them, An <u>enemy hath done this.</u> The servants said unto him, Wilt thou then that we go and gather them up?

29. But he said, <u>Nay;</u> lest while ye <u>gather up the tares, ye root up also the wheat with them.</u>

30. Let <u>both grow together until the harvest:</u> and in the time of harvest I will say to the reapers, Gather ye together <u>first the tares, and bind them in bundles to burn them: but gather the wheat into my barn</u>. (KJV)

Our Lord Jesus Christ went on to explain this parable to his disciples.

Matt. 13:34-43

34. All these things spake Jesus unto the multitude in parables; and without a parable spake he not unto them:

35. That it might be fulfilled which was spoken by the prophet, saying, I will open my mouth in parables; I will <u>utter things which have been kept secret from the foundation of the world.</u>

36. Then Jesus sent the multitude away, and went into the house: and his disciples came unto him, saying, Declare unto us the parable of the tares of the field.

37. He answered and said unto them, He that soweth the good seed is the Son of man;

38. The <u>fields is the world; the good seed are the children of the kingdom; but the tares are the children of the wicked one;</u>

39. <u>The enemy that sowed them is the devil;</u> the <u>harvest is the</u> end of the <u>world;</u> and the <u>reapers are the angels.</u>

40. As therefore the <u>tares are gathered and burned in the fire;</u> so shall it be in the <u>end of this world.</u>

41. The Son of man shall <u>send forth his an-gels,</u> and they <u>shall gather out</u> out of his kingdom all things <u>that offend,</u> and them which <u>do iniquity;</u>

42. And shall <u>cast them into a furnace of fire:</u> there shall be wailing and gnashing of teeth.

43. <u>Then shall the righteous shine forth as the sun in the kingdom of their Father. Who hath ears to hear, let him hear.</u>

Verse 35 was taken from Psalms, which is what the Old Testament was all about concerning the New.

Ps. 78:2-4

24. I will <u>open my mouth in a parable:</u> I will <u>utter dark sayings of old;</u>

25. Which we have <u>heard and known, and our fathers have told us.</u>

26. We will not hide them from their children, <u>shewing to the generation that he hath done.</u> (KJV)

Verse 3 says that we have known what our fathers knew. This is so true, as we look at our examples of things to come. The Psalmist goes on to say that these things will happen, so we can put our faith in him who is the author, and finisher, of our faith (Hebrews 12:2). Paul writes in 1 Corinthians 14:3 that God is not the author of confusion.

So all things are clear, as we look at the word, and with the help of the Holy Spirit, all things will be understood. So looking at the parable of the tares, does this look like the saints will be gone first? No, they will be here until the end, and then be gathered into his kingdom, and have eternal life with Christ. More on this subject in another chapter.

The Churches of Revelation

Now that the background has been laid, we will look at the churches themselves, as revealed in Revelation chapters 2 and 3. These are the churches in the end times. The use of the old Asiatic church names is only a type, and is characteristics of using names like the beast to portray Satan's one- world system in Revelation and Daniel. As we go through these various churches, we will see that they are end time prophecies. John, when writing to the seven churches, had this to say.

Rev. 1:4

4. John to the seven churches which are in Asia: Grace be unto you, and peace, from him which is, and which was, and which is to come; and from the <u>seven Spirits which are before his throne</u>; (KJV)

This message was to be sent to the seven churches, so as the word could be disseminated throughout the Christian world. The time in which all the events of Revelation takes place is recorded in this manner.

Rev. 1:10

10. I was in <u>the Spirit on the Lord's day,</u> and heard behind me a great voice, as of a trumpet, (KJV)

Some would have you believe that John was talking about Sunday, as the Church today considers this the Lord's Day. This is a misnomer, as the original Sabbath was on a Saturday, or the seventh day of the week. Sunday, being the first day of the week, started being celebrated as the Sabbath after Constantine took power of the Roman Empire, and established the Nicaea Council. So Sunday could not be the day that John was talking about. Was it the original Sabbath? No. You see, John was a disciple of Jesus and he knew the teachings of Christ concerning the Sabbath.

Mark 2:28

28. Therefore the <u>Son of man is Lord also of the sabbath.</u>

Luke 6:5

5. And he said unto them, <u>That the Son of man is Lord also of the sabbath.</u> (KJV)

The fact that Christ is the Lord of the Sabbath, indicates that he is the Sabbath. The word **Sabbath** in the Hebrew has this meaning:

7673 shabath (shaw-bath');
a primitive root; to repose, i.e., <u>desist from exertion;</u> used in many implied relations (causative, figurative or specific):

As God rested on the Sabbath, after he made the world, so was man to rest on the seventh day. When Christ became Lord of the Sabbath, he became our rest. We should observe the Sabbath, or rest in Christ. Then John was not talking about a specific day of the week, when he said the Lord's Day. What he was talking about was the end times, which are referred to as "The Day of the Lord," "That Great Day of the Lord" or as John simply put it, "The Lord's Day," which is when Christ will come to rule and reign here on earth.

So all the events in Revelation are pertaining to end-time prophecy, from chapter 1 to 22. Looking then at the churches, in chapters 2 and 3, they are end-time churches. There were only two of the end-time churches that Jesus did not find fault with. What did they know that caused them to be faultless? Let's take a look, and see who and what they did.

Rev. 2:8-11

8. And unto the angel of the church in Smyrna write; These things saith the first and the last, which was dead, and is alive;

9. I know thy works, and tribulation, and poverty, (but thou art rich) <u>I know the blasphemy of them which say they are Jews, and are not, but are the synagogue of Satan.</u>

10. Fear none of those things which thou shalt suffer: behold, the <u>devil shall cast some of you into prison,</u> that ye may be tried; and ye shall have tribulation ten days: be <u>thou faithful unto death,</u> and I will <u>give thee a</u>

<u>crown of life.</u>

11. He that hath an ear, let him hear what the Spirit saith unto the churches; <u>He that overcometh shall not be hurt of the second death</u>. (KJV)

Verse 9 states that Christ knows the blasphemy of them which say they are Jews, and are not, but are the synagogue of Satan. We know that Satan will come as Christ and will set up his kingdom in Jerusalem, as Christ will in his Second coming.

So the Antichrist will say as well that his followers are Jews or of Judah, but they are not. They are of Satan, not of Judah. To say otherwise is blasphemy. This part of the Church will know the truth, that Satan is on the scene, not Christ. The second church has similar characteristics.

Rev. 3:7-13

7. And to the angel of the church in Philadelphia write; These things saith he that is holy, he that is true, he that hath the key of David, he that openeth, and no man shutteth; and shutteth, and no man openeth;

8. I know thy works: behold, I have set before thee an open door, and no man can shut it: for thou hast a little strength, and hast kept my word, and hast not denied my name.

9. <u>Behold, I will make them of the synagogue of Satan, which say they are Jews, and are not, but do lie; behold, I will make them to come and worship before thy feet, and to</u>

<u>know that I have loved thee.</u>

10. Because thou hast kept the word of my patience, I also will keep thee from the hour of temptation, which shall come upon all the world, to try them that dwell upon the earth.

11. Behold, I come quickly: hold that fast which thou hast, that no man take thy crown.

12. <u>Him that overcometh will I make a pillar in the temple of my God,</u> and he shall go no more out: and I will write upon him the name of my God, and the name of the city of my God, which is new Jerusalem, which cometh down out of heaven from my God: and I will write upon him my new name.

13. <u>He that hath an ear, let him hear what the Spirit saith unto the churches</u>. (KJV)

Verse 9 also talks about the synagogues of Satan. These, by this definition, can only be end-time churches. We know that the spirit of Antichrist has ruled throughout history, even in John's day, but his actual appearance in the synagogue will not be until the end time. Keeping Christ's commandments, and knowing the truth, that Satan will rule before Christ comes, and recognizing him in his synagogue, while he is on earth, is what our Lord does not find fault with. What was the problem with the other five churches and why did Jesus find fault in them?

Rev. 2:1-7

1. Unto the angel of the church of Ephesus

write; These things saith he that holdeth the seven stars in his right hand, who walketh in the midst of the seven golden candlesticks;

2. <u>I know thy works, and thy labour, and thy patience,</u> and how thou <u>canst not bear them which are evil:</u> and thou <u>hast tried them which say they are apostles, and are not, and hast found</u> them liars:

3. <u>And hast borne, and hast patience, and for my name's sake hast</u> laboured, and hast not fainted.

4. <u>Nevertheless I have somewhat against thee,</u> because thou hast <u>left</u> thy <u>first love.</u>

5. <u>Remember therefore from whence thou art fallen, and repent,</u> and do the first works; or else I will come unto thee quickly, and will remove thy candlestick out of his place, except thou repent.

6. But this thou hast, that thou hatest the deeds of the Nicolaitans, which I also hate.

7. He that hath an ear, let him hear what the Spirit saith unto the churches; To him that overcometh will I give to eat of the tree of life, which is in the midst of the paradise of God. (KJV)

We will look at the word **left** in verse 4.

863 aphiemi (af-ee'-ay-mee);
from 575 and hiemi <u>(to send;</u> an intensive form of eimi, <u>to to);</u> to send forth, in various applications (as follow):

To further amplify this meaning, let's break this down to its prime root.

575 apo (apo');
a primary particle; "of," i.e., <u>away</u> (from something near), in various senses (of place, time, or <u>relation;</u> literal or figurative):

So the church has separated or departed from its first love, which was Christ, and has looked upon Satan as Christ, and believed his deception that he has come down to rule on earth. This is why "The Great Tribulation" will be like no other in the past or future. We as Christians need the whole armor of God, as stated by Paul.

Eph. 6:11-13

11. <u>Put on the whole armour of God,</u> that ye may be able to stand against the wiles of the devil.

12. For we wrestle not against flesh and blood, but against principalities, against powers, against the rulers of the darkness of this world, against spiritual wickedness in high places.

13. Wherefore take unto you the whole armour of God, that ye may be able to <u>withstand in the evil day,</u> and having done all, to stand. (KJV)

Verse 13 specifically states <u>"to withstand in the evil day,"</u> which is Satan's day. Make no mistake that it will be easy, but with the Holy Spirit as your guide, and the armor of Salvation, you can prevail.

The next church with which our Lord finds fault is as follows.

Rev. 2:12-17

12. And to the angel of the church in Pergamos write; These things saith he which hath the sharp sword with two edges;

13. I know thy works, and <u>where thou dwellest, even where Satan's seat is:</u> and thou holdest fast my name, and hast not denied my faith, even in those days wherein Antipas was my faithful martyr, who was slain among you, where Satan dwelleth.

14. But I have a <u>few things against thee, because thou hast there them that hold the doctrine of Balaam, who taught Balac to cast a stumblingblock before the children of Israel, to eat things sacrificed unto idols, and to commit fornication.</u>

15. So hast thou also them that hold the <u>doctrine of the Nicolaitans,</u> which thing I hate.

16. Repent; or else I will come unto thee quickly, and will fight against them with the sword of my mouth_

17. He that hath an ear, let him hear what the Spirit saith unto the churches; <u>To him that overcometh will I give to eat of the hidden manna, and will give him a white stone, and in the stone a new name written, which no man knoweth saving he that receiveth it</u>. (KJV)

In verse 14 we see that in this end-time church, some will follow the doctrine of Balaam, to cast a stumbling block before the children of Israel, which is the church grafted in. What happened to Israel, will happen to the churches of the end times.

Num. 25:1-2

1. And Israel abode in Shittim, and the people began to commit whoredom with the daughters of Moab.

2. And they <u>called the people unto the sacrifices of their gods: and the people did eat, and bowed down to their gods</u>. (KJV)

Bowing down to their gods, the ones that are not the true Messiah. We see how history will repeat itself. As it was in the days of Israel of old, so shall it be in the latter days. Verse 15 talks about the doctrine of the Nicolaitans. This is unclear in Scripture and is only used in Revelation. *Thayer's* definition defines Nicolaitans as follows.

3531 Nikolaites-
Nicolaitans = <u>"destruction of people"</u> ;
a sect mentioned in Rev. 2:6,15, who were charged with holding the error of Balaam, casting a stumbling block in front of the ekklesia of God by upholding the liberty of eating things sacrificed to idols as well as committing fornication

The meaning of Nicolaitans, to be "destruction of people," is the best definition we can find, as this doctrine will lead people to go away from their first love of Christ, and worship Antichrist.

The third church mentioned in Revelation is Thyatira. Let's see what the Scripture has to say about their fault.

Rev. 2:18-29

18. And unto the angel of the church in Thyatira write; These things saith the Son of God, who hath his eyes like unto a flame of fire, and his feet are like fine brass;

19. I know thy words, and charity, and service, and faith, and thy patience, and thy works; and the last to be more than the first.

20. Notwithstanding <u>I have a few things against thee, because thou sufferest that woman Jezebel, which calleth herself a prophetess, to teach and to seduce my servants to commit fornication, and to eat things sacrificed</u> unto idols.

21. And I gave her space to repent of her fornication; and she repented not.

22. Behold, I will cast her into a bed, and them that commit adultery with her into great tribulation, except they repent of their deeds.

23. And I will kill her children with death; and all the churches shall know that I am he which searcheth the reins and hearts: and I will give unto every one of you according to your works.

24. But unto you I say, and unto the rest in Thyatira, <u>as many as have not this doc-</u>

trine, and which have not known the depths of Satan, as they speak; I will put upon you none other burden.

25. But that which ye have already hold fast till I come.

26. And he that overcometh, and keepeth my works unto the end, to him will I give power over the nations :

27. And he shall rule them with a rod of iron; as the vessels of a potter shall they be broken to shivers: even as I received of my father.

28. And I will give him the morning star.

29. He that hath an ear, let him hear what the Spirit saith unto the churches. (KJV)

We see that the fault was the false prophetess Jezebel. From reading the word, we know that Jezebel lived during Elijah's time. This is only another symbolic sign of the end times. We read in the Book of Malachi this passage concerning Elijah:

Mal. 4:5

5. Behold, I will send you Elijah the prophet before the coming of the great and dreadful day of the LORD: (KJV)

We know that in different times of Jesus's ministry, the Scribes and Pharisees asked him if he was Elijah, which was to come. In Matthew we read an account of Jesus being asked about Elijah, and John the Baptist.

Was Christ Really an Angel or Reincarnated?

Matt. 11:11-15

11. Verily I say unto you, Among them that are born of women there hath not risen a greater than John the Baptist: notwithstanding <u>he that is least in</u> the kingdom of heaven is greater than he.

12. And from the days of John the Baptist until now the kingdom of heaven suffereth violence, and the violent take it by force.

13. For all the prophets and the law prophesied until John.

14. <u>And if ye will receive it, this is Elias, which was for to come.</u>

15. He that hath ears to hear, let him hear. (KJV)

In verse 11 some have taken it out of context. All kinds of thoughts have been brought forth. Some will say that by the saying, "he that is least in the kingdom of heaven is greater than he," proves that Christ is an angel. But the word **angel** is not used in this verse. Everywhere the word **angel** or angels is used, *Strong's Concordance* number was 4397, which means the following:

4397 mar ak (mal-awk');
from an unused root meaning to despatch as a deputy; <u>a messenger;</u> specifically, of God, i.e., <u>an angel</u> (also a prophet, priest or teacher):

But in Psalm 8:5, we have the following

meaning:

Ps. 8:5

5. For thou hast <u>made him a little lower than the angels,</u> and hast <u>crowned him with glory and honour</u>. (KJV)

For the word **angels,** *Strong's Concordance* has this meaning:

430 'elohiym (el-o-heem');
<u>plural</u> of 433; gods in the ordinary sense; but specifically used (in the plural thus, <u>especially with the article) of the supreme God;</u> occasionally applied by way of deference to magistrates; and sometimes as a superlative:

This verse in the Psalms shows that Christ was God. Christ's statement was simply that as great as John was, Christ becoming a man in his reduced state, was still greater than John the Baptist. Those religions and organizations that believe Christ was an angel are the furthest from the truth, because this verse proves alone that Christ is God. Let's look in the book of Hebrews.

Heb. 1:3-10

3. Who being the brightness of his glory, and <u>the express image</u> of his <u>person,</u> and upholding all things by the word of his power, when he had by himself purged our sins, sat down on the right hand of the Majesty on high:

4. Being made so much better than the angels, as he hath by inheritance obtained a more excellent name than they.

5. <u>For unto which of the angels said he at any time. Thou art my Son, this day have I begotten thee? And again, I will be to him a Father, and he shall be to me a Son?</u>

6. And again, when he bringeth in the first begotten into the world, he saith, <u>And let all the angels of God worship him.</u>

7. And of the angels he saith, <u>Who maketh his angels spirits,</u> and his ministers a flame of fire.

8. But <u>unto the Son he saith, Thy throne, O God, is for ever and ever: a sceptre of righteousness is the sceptre of thy kingdom.</u>

9. Thou hast loved righteousness, and hated iniquity; therefore God, even thy God, hath anointed thee with the oil of gladness above thy fellows.

10. And, <u>Thou, Lord, in the beginning hast laid the foundation of the earth; and the heavens are the works of thine hands</u>: (KJV)

Therefore in this vein of truth, it should become more obvious, in the written word of Hebrews chapter 2:

Heb. 2:5-9

5. For unto the angels hath he not put in subjection the world to come, whereof we speak.

6. <u>But one in a certain place testified, saying, What is man, that thou art mindful of him? or the son of man, that thou visitest him?</u>

7. <u>Thou madest him a little lower than the</u>

angels; thou crownedst him with glory and honour, and didst set him over the works of thy hands:

8. Thou hast put all things in subjection under his feet. For in that he put all in subjection under him, he left nothing that is not put under him. But now we see not yet all things put under him.

9. But we see Jesus, who was made a little lower than the angels for the suffering of death, crowned with glory and honour; that he by the grace of God should taste death for every man. (KJV)

Another misunderstood verse about Jesus not being equal with the Father, is found in the Book of John. This verse gives the impression that Jesus does not have equality with the Father. Let's examine what Jesus meant by the word **greater.**

John 14:28

28. Ye have heard how I said unto you, I go away, and come again unto you. If ye loved me, ye would rejoice, because J said, J go unto the Father: for my Father is greater than I. (KJV)

The word *greater* has the following meaning.

3187 meizon (mide'-zone);
irregular comparative of 3173; larger (literally or figuratively, *specifically in age):*

The underlined meanings indicate that Christ was talking about an irregular comparative, which specifically dealt with size, not quality or essence of his being. Now if Jesus meant that he was less than God in quality or essence, he would have used the word **greater** found in Matthew.

Matt. 12:41

41. The men of Nineveh shall rise in judgment with this generation, and shall condemn it: because they repented at the preaching of Jonas; and, behold, a <u>greater</u> than Jonas is here. (KJV)

This **greater** will show a qualitative difference of being less than equal or inferior to the other.

4119 pleion (pli-own);
neuter pleion (pli'- on); or pleon (pleh'- on); comparative of 4183; <u>more in quantity,</u> number, <u>or quality;</u> also (in plural) the major portion:
KJV—X above, + exceed, <u>more excellent,</u> further, (very) great (- er), long (- er), (very) many, greater (more) part, + yet but.

Here is quite evident that Jesus' comment concerning Jonah was an absolute superior state of being, edified by meaning <u>more excellent.</u> To use an analogy of what is being expressed in the comparison that Jesus used about him and the Father, think of a thousand- pound block of solid gold. If you were to cut off one ounce from the block, in essence, the one ounce is still as pure as the block that it was taken from. So the ounce of gold is still the same as the block from which it was taken.

Now let's go back to verse 14 of Matthew 11. Jesus says that "if ye receive it, this is Elias."

What Jesus was talking about was, that if they had received him as Messiah, then John the Baptist would have been Elias or Elijah, but as they did not receive him. Then Elijah was to come in the end times before his coming.

The authors feel that Elijah is one of the two witnesses spoken of in Revelation and Enoch the other, as they did not die, but were translated up to haven.

So Jezebel represents to the church during the end times, as she did in the ancient times, destruction of all that was good and teach the church to commit fornication with Antichrist. It also says her children will be killed, this is in reference to the ones who follow her. We are talking about Satan all through these churches and that he is physically here on earth. So the churches in which Christ finds fault have some elements that will try to lead many believers astray. The next church, Sardis, has some faults also.

Rev. 3:1-6

1. And unto the angel of the church in Sardis write, These things saith he that hath the seven Spirits of God, and the seven stars; I know thy works, that thou hast a name that thou livest, and art dead.

2. Be watchful, and strengthen the things which remain, that are ready to die for: <u>for I have not found thy works perfect before God.</u>

3. Remember therefore how thou hast received and heard, and hold fast, and re-

pent. If therefore thou shalt not watch, I will come on thee as a thief, and thou shalt not know what hour I will come upon thee.

4.   Thou hast a few names even in Sardis which have <u>not defiled their garments;</u> and they shall <u>walk with me in white;</u> for they are worthy.

5.   He that <u>overcometh, the same shall be clothed in white raiment;</u> and I will <u>not blot out his name out of the book of life,</u> but I will confess his name before my Father, and before his angels.

6.   He that hath an ear, let him hear what the Spirit saith unto the churches. (KJV)

This church, in verse 2, Christ found their works not perfect before God. The word *perfect* has this meaning in the Greek.

4137 pleroo (play-ro'-o);
from 4134; <u>to make replete,</u> i.e., (literally) to cram (a net), <u>level</u> up (a hallow), or (figuratively) to <u>furnish (or imbue, diffuse, influences),</u> <u>satisfy, execute (an office), finish (a period or task),</u> verify (or coincide with a prediction), etc.:

The word *replete* means "fully provided." In other words they were not fully clothed with the whole armor of God, and not ready to stand up to Antichrist. The word *imbue* has an interesting meaning.

1.   To inspire, permeate, or <u>invade: work imbued with the revolutionary spirit.</u> See Synonyms at CHARGE.

This definition implies that some in this church were not inspired by the word, and did not help others to take a stand in these troubled times. They also did not execute their office in the church, by teaching false doctrines and making some to take Antichrist as Christ himself. Also in this verse it says that a few in this church did hold fast, and kept their garments white. This is why we as Christians need to search the Word of God for his truth, and not man's.

The fifth church for which Christ finds fault is in their belief, which encompasses a lot of believers today. We find a lot of churches that seem to sit on the fence and see which way the wind is blowing to decide which 'way to go. Christ describes them like this.

Rev. 3:14-22

14. And unto the angel of the church of the Laodiceans write; These things saith the Amen, the faithful and true witness, the beginning of the creation of God;

15. I know thy works, that thou art neither cold nor hot: I would thou wert cold or hot.

16. So then because thou art lukewarm, and neither cold nor hot, I will spue thee out of my mouth.

17. Because thou sayest, I am rich, and increased with goods, and have need of nothing; and knowest not that thou art wretched, and miserable, and poor, and blind, and naked:

18. I counsel thee to buy of me gold tried in the fire, that thou mayest be rich; and

white raiment, that thou mayest be clothed, and that the shame of thy nakedness do not appear; and anoint thine eyes with eyesalve, that thou mayest see.

19. <u>As many as I love, I rebuke and chasten: be zealous therefore, and repent.</u>

20. <u>Behold, I stand at the door, and knock: if any man hear my voice, and open the door, I will come in to him, and will sup with him, and he with me.</u>

21. To him <u>that overcometh will I grant to sit with me in my throne,</u> even as <u>I also overcame,</u> and am set down with my Father in his throne.

22. He that <u>hath an ear, let him hear what the Spirit saith unto the churches.</u> (KJV)

In verse 15 John writes that this church, is <u>neither "hot or cold,"</u> but "lukewarm." Our Lord says that because they are neither hot or cold he will spew them out of his mouth. As we read further, we see in verse 17 that this church is rich with material goods, and they need nothing. Some Christians only go to church because they think that this is the way to let people know they are good people. We get in our comfort zones when we have plenty, and do not seek God and his righteousness, and just look at our own selves. We say to ourselves, we have plenty; therefore God must be taking care of us. It is written that we should seek first the Kingdom of God and then all these things shall be added unto us (Matt. 6:33).

Verse 18 says that "counsel thee to buy of me gold tried in the fire, that thou mayest be rich."

This is not physical gold but spiritual gold. Paul says it better than we could when he was speaking to the Corinthians.

1 Cor. 3:13-15

13. Every man's work shall be made manifest: for the day shall declare it, because it <u>shall be revealed by fire;</u> and the <u>fire shall try every man's work of what sort it is.</u>

14. If any man's work abide which he hath built thereupon, he shall receive a reward.

15. If any man's work shall be burned, he shall suffer loss: but he himself shall be saved; yet so as by fire. (KJV)

Peter also talks about being tried in the fire, as follows:

1 Pet. 1:7

7. <u>That the trial of your faith, being much more precious than of gold that perisheth, though it be tried with fire, might be found unto praise and honour and glory at the appearing of Jesus Christ</u>: (KJV)

In verse 19 of Revelation, Christ goes on to say that if we are tried in the fire then we will be rich, with white raiment, which is far more precious than any gold this earth has to offer. Paul and Peter talk about faith being tried in the fire.

John also states to the church that we should anoint our eyes with eyesalve, that we may see. This eyesalve is the Holy Spirit, who will let us see the true meanings of God word, if we study in deep prayer looking for the truth. Verse 22 says that all these verses on the churches end with this statement: "He that hath an ear let him hear what the Spirit says to the churches." Jesus, when asked why he spake in parables, answered thus.

Matt. 13:13

13. <u>Therefore speak J to them in parables: because they seeing see not; and hearing they hear not, neither do they understand</u>. (KJV)

If Christians do not tune their eyes and ears to the truth, they will not be prepared for that final day of the Lord, as Ezekiel says, to prepare us to stand in the battle in the day of the Lord (Ezek. 13:5).

To sum up the churches, we see that the two churches that Christ found no fault in knew that Satan was in the synagogue pretending to be of Judah, which we know he is not. They recognized who Antichrist really was. The other churches had people who did not know the truth and were worshiping Satan. The lukewarm Christians are neither hot nor cold, those who have plenty, who do not take their Christianity seriously. What we need in these end times is a turning back to the true word of God, searching his Scriptures for the truth and not listening to the traditions of men.

In the next chapter, we will go further into the teaching of traditions and how they have affected the church today.

7

The Traditions of Men Being Taught in the Church

Judah and Israel

In teaching God's word there is one point that we feel the Church has completely overlooked, with a few exceptions. This fact is that Israel and Judah or the Jews have been lumped into one group. Every time Israel is mentioned by most teachers of the word, they usually mention the Jews, with the same meaning. Scripture is very clear that these are two different groups of people. The kingdom was divided when David ascended to the throne. We have an account of this in 2 Samuel.

2 Sam. 5:4-5

4.   David was thirty years old when he began to reign, and he reigned forty years.

5.   In Hebron <u>he reigned over Judah seven years and six months:</u> and in Jerusalem he <u>reigned thirty and three years over all Israel and Judah</u>. (KJV)

So we see that David united the kingdom after seven years of reign over Judah. After David died, his son Solomon assumed the throne. Now Solomon sinned against God by worshiping the idols of his wives. In 1 Kings we get the following account of what God decreed to Solomon for his sins:

1 Kings 11:9-13

9.   And the LORD was angry with Solomon, because his heart was turned from the LORD God of Israel, which had appeared unto him twice,

10. And had commanded him concerning this thing, that he should not go after other gods: but he kept not that which the LORD commanded.

11. Wherefore the LORD said unto Solomon, Forasmuch as this is done of thee, and thou bast not kept my covenant and my statutes, which I have commanded thee, I will surely rend the kingdom from thee, and will give it to thy servant.

12. Notwithstanding in thy days I will not do it for David thy father's sake: but I will rend it out of the hand of thy son.

13. Howbeit I will not rend away all the kingdom; but will give one tribe to thy son for David my servant's sake and for Jerusalem's sake which I have chosen. (KJV)

Verse 13 states that all of the kingdom would not be taken from Solomon's son, and Jerusalem would remain the capital of Judah. This story unfolds later in 1 Kings where Jeroboam was anointed King of Israel.

1 Kings 11:28-37

28. And the man Jeroboam was a mighty man of valour: and Solomon seeing the young

man that he was industrious, <u>he made him ruler over</u> all the charge of the <u>house of Joseph.</u>

29. And it came to pass at that time when Jeroboam went out of Jerusalem, that the prophet Ahijah the Shilonite found him in the way; and he had clad himself with a new garment; and they two were alone in the field:

30. And Ahijah caught the new garment that was on him, and rent it in twelve pieces:

31. And he said to Jeroboam, Take thee ten pieces: for thus saith the LORD, the God of Israel, Behold, <u>I will rend the kingdom</u> out of the hand of <u>Solomon, and will</u> give ten tribes to thee:

32. But he shall have <u>one tribe for my servant David's sake, and for Jerusalem's sake, the city which I have chosen out of all the tribes of Israel:</u>

33. Because that they have forsaken me, and have worshiped Ashtoreth the goddess of the Zidonians, Chemosh the god of the Morabites, and Milcom the god of the children of Ammon, and have not walked in my ways, to do that which is right in mine eyes, and to keep my statutes and my judgments, as did David his father.

34. Howbeit I will <u>not take the whole kingddom out of his hand:</u> but I will make him prince all the days of his life for David my servant's sake, whom I chose, because lie kept my commandments and my statutes:

35. <u>But I will take the kingddom out of his son's hand, and will give it unto thee, even ten tribes.</u>

36. And unto <u>his son will I give one tribe,</u> that David my servant may have a light alway before me in Jerusalem, the city which I have chosen me to put my name there.

37. <u>And I will take thee, and thou shalt reign according to all that thy soul desireth, and shalt be king over Israel.</u> (KJV)

Verse 28 is interesting as Solomon put Jeroboam over the house of Joseph. The word *house* has this meaning in the Hebrew.

1004 bayith (bah'-yith);
probably from 1129 abbreviated; a house (in the greatest variation of applications, <u>especially family,</u> etc.):

In reality we know that it was not a physical house that you live in, but a family of people. So Joseph's ancestry would be over the house of Israel. This is confirmed in 1 Chronicles.

1 Chron. 5:1-2

1. Now the sons of Reuben <u>the firstborn of Israel,</u> (for he was the firstborn; but, <u>forasmuch as he defiled his father's bed, his birthright was given unto the sons of Joseph the son of Israel:</u> and the genealogy is not to be reckoned after the birthright.

2. For <u>Judah prevailed above his brethen, and of him came the chief ruler; but the birthright was Joseph's :)</u>

Judah was given the kingship, but Joseph

was given the birthright. We see Judah's kingship in Genesis when Jacob blesses his children.

Gen. 49:8-10

8. Judah, thou art he whom thy brethren shall praise: thy hand shall be in the neck of time enemies; thy father's children shall bow down before thee.

9. Judah is a lion's whelp: from the prey, my son, thou art gone up: he stooped down, he couched as a lion, and as an old lion; who shall rouse him up?

10. The sceptre shall not depart from Judah, nor a lawgiver from between his feet, until Shiloh come; arid unto him shall the gathering of the people be. (KJV)

Here we see that the sceptre or kingship will not depart from Judah, nor a lawgiver from between his feet. This gives the tribe of Judah the kingship. Saul was from the tribe of Benjamin and God reluctantly gave the children of Israel to Saul as their king. But David was from the tribe of Judah. It goes on to say "until Shiloh come." This is the meaning of Shiloh.

7886 Shiyloh (shee-lo');
from 7951; tranquil; Shiloh, an epithet of the Messiah:

Some think that this took place when Christ first came to earth. This is also end-time prophecy because this is when Jesus returns and gathers his people unto him. Now the birthright was passed on to Joseph, which Israel passed on to Ephraim when he blessed Joseph's two sons. Let's look at Joseph's blessing from his father.

Gen. 49:22-24

22. Joseph is a fruitful bough, even a fruitful bough by a well; whose branches run over the wall:

23. The archers have sorely grieved him, and shot at him, and hated him:

24. But his bow abode in strength, and the arms of his hands were made strong by the hands of the mighty God of Jacob; (from thence is the shepherd, the stone of Israel:) (KJV)

Joseph was the shepherd, the stone of Israel according to verse 24. We read elsewhere the kingdoms were divided during the first part of David's reign, and then united. After Solomon died, they were divided, Israel to the north and Judah and Benjamin to the south. In Ezekiel God tells the prophet, who primarily was a prophet to the house of Israel, about the two kingdoms. Remember *house* means family.

Ezek. 23:1-4

1. The word of the LORD came again unto me, saying,

2. Son of man, there were two women, the daughters of one another:

3. And they committed whoredoms in Egypt; they committed whoredoms in their youth: there were their breasts pressed, and there they bruised the teats of their virginity.

4. And the names of them were Aholah the elder, and Aholibah her sister: and they were mine, and they bare sons and daugh-

ters. Thus were their names; <u>Samaria is Aholah,</u> and <u>Jerusalem Aholibah</u>. (KJV)

Here God says he saw two sisters even while they were in Egypt. We know that Samaria was the northern kingdom and Judea the southern part. In reading the accounts of each in 1 & 2 Kings and 1 & 2 Chronicles, we well see how they fought each other, but they also defended each other at times, because they knew they were brothers.

To understand why there is a <u>difference between the books of Kings and Chronicles,</u> you have to understand that the Book of Kings was written history according to the <u>northern kingdom Israel.</u> The book of Chronicles was written <u>history according to the southern kingdom of Judah.</u>

We know from history that the house of Israel was taken into captivity by Assyria long before Judah was taken by Babylon. In the Book of Hosea, who was also a prophet to the northern kingdom of Israel, we see in the first chapter how God would disperse the children of Israel.

Hosea 1:2-11

2. The beginning of the word of the LORD by Hosea. And the LORD said to Hosea, Go, take unto thee a wife of whoredoms and children of whoredoms: <u>for the land hath committed great whoredom, departing from the LORD.</u>

3. So he went and took Gomer the daughter of Diblaim; which conceived, and bare him a son.

4. And the LORD said unto him, Call his name <u>Jezreel;</u> for yet a little while, and I will avenge the <u>blood of Jezreel upon the house of Jehu,</u> and will cause to <u>cease the king-dom of the house of Israel.</u>

5. And it shall come to pass at that day, that <u>I will break the bow of Israel in the valley of Jezreel.</u>

6. And she conceived again, and bare a daughter. And God said unto him, Call her name <u>Loruhamah:</u> for <u>I will no more have mercy upon the house of Israel; but I will utterly take them away.</u>

7. <u>But I will have mercy upon the house of Ju-dah,</u> and will save them by the LORD their God, and will not save them by bow, nor by sword, nor by battle, by horses, nor by horsemen.

8. Now when she had weaned <u>Loruhamah,</u> she conceived, and bare a son.

9. <u>Then said God. Call his name Loammi: for ye are not my people, and I will not be your God.</u>

10. <u>Yet the number of the children of Israel shall be as the sand of the sea, which can-not be measured nor numbered; and it shall come to pass, that in the place where it was said unto them, Ye are not</u> my peo-ple, there it shall be said unto them, Ye are the sons of the living God.

11. Then shall the children of <u>Judah and the children of Israel be gathered together,</u> and appoint themselves one head, and they

shall come up out of the land: for great shall be the day of Jezreel. (KJV)

So Israel did indeed commit great sins against the Lord, by worshiping idols, and for this God was going to disperse them. The first child born of this relationship, which God ordered was named Jezreel. In God's dealings with his people, he used a man named Jehu to bring about his judgments. But he did not do according to God's plan. You can read about this in 2 Kings 9- 10.

The second child born was named Lo-ruhamah, which means, <u>God will not have mercy upon the House of Israel.</u> God went on to say that he <u>would have mercy upon the house of Judah</u> and will save them.

The third child born was called Lo- ammi, which means, <u>not my people.</u> Now if God divorced Israel so to speak, then what happened to them? Verse 10 is a very misunderstood section that says that wherever they go, they would be like the sand of the sea, which cannot be numbered. It also says that wherever they are, even though they are not his people, they will be known as the <u>sons of the living God.</u> So Israel was scattered in the world, and by their numbers are exceedingly populous.

They <u>do not know who they are,</u> but they will when Christ comes and he will <u>gather up Judah and Israel together</u> and plant them back in their own land.

To <u>say that Israel and Judah, or the Jews, are synonymous is another church tradition that has</u>

no foundation and is contrary to God's word. This is why some prophecy teachers err in their teaching, because when the Bible talks of Israel, they think that this is the Jews or the tribe of Judah. We will not get into the theories concerning the lost ten tribes, but we will state that not all Israelites are Jews, but all Jews are Israelites, because they were united, they were all called Israelites, which comes from Jacob, who was renamed Israel. All Israelites are considered Gentiles according to the meaning as being non-Jewish. This does not mean that all Gentiles are of the ten tribes.

It is important when looking at prophecies concerning Judah and Israel that we remember the difference, because some prophecies are different, depending on who is addressed. When we see the term "the House of Israel" used, it is pertaining to the northern kingdoms. The House of Judah pertains to the southern tribes of Judah and Benjamin.

The Speaking in an Unknown Tongue

Another tradition that we will get into is speaking in an unknown tongue. A lot of evangelic al churches adhere to this tradition. Let's look at Acts chapter 2 and see what was said about the tongue spoken on Pentecost Day.

Acts 2:1-13

1. And when the day of Pentecost was fully come, they were all with one accord in one place.

2. And suddenly there came a sound from heaven as of a rushing mighty wind, and it

filled all the house where they were sitting.

3. And there <u>appeared unto them cloven tongues like as of fire, and it sat upon each of them.</u>

4. And they were <u>all filled with the Holy Ghost,</u> and <u>began to speak with other tongues, as the Spirit gave them utterance.</u>

5. And there were dwelling at Jerusalem <u>Jews,</u> devout men, out <u>of every nation under heaven.</u>

6. Now when this was noised abroad, the multitude came together, and <u>were confounded, because that every man heard them speak in his own language.</u>

7. And they were all amazed and marvelled, saying one to another, Behold, <u>are not all these which speak Galilaeans?</u>

8. <u>And how hear we every man in our own tongue, wherein we were born?</u>

9. Parthians, and Medes, and Elamites, and the dwellers in Mesopotamia, and in Judaea, and Cappadocia, in Pontus, and Asia,

10. Phrygia, and Pamphylia, in Egypt, and in the parts of Libya about Cyrene, and strangers of Rome, Jews and proselytes,

11. Cretes and Arabians, we do hear them speak in our tongues the wonderful works of God.

12. And they were all amazed, and were in doubt, saying one to another, What meaneth this?

13. Others mocking said, These men are full of
    new wine. (KJV)

The first verse depicts the <u>true meaning of
worshiping in the Holy Spirit,</u> because it states
they were <u>all in one accord.</u> This is important:
the <u>Church be of one mind</u> and not off <u>into different ways of worshiping. Too many different
doctrines</u> are being taught in the Church today.
This is why we have so many <u>different denominations.</u> Paul criticized the Church for its sepa-
rations in 1 Corinthians.

1 Cor. 1:12-13

12. Now this I say, that every one of you saith,
    <u>I am of Paul; and I of Apollos; and I of
    Cephas; and I of Christ.</u>

13. <u>Is Christ divided?</u> was Paul crucified for
    you? or were ye baptized in the name of
    Paul? (KJV)

No, Christ is not divided, but is <u>one body</u> and
should be in one accord.

Now as we look more at the second chapter
of Acts, we see that there was a sound from
heaven, as a rushing mighty wind. Is this being
<u>heard in the churches today?</u> If so then we have
never heard of it, let alone seen cloven tongues
of fire appearing before men.

Now there were men of Judah who had been
scattered to all parts of the earth <u>speaking different languages or tongues,</u> who had come to
Jerusalem to observe the feast of Pentecost.
When they heard of what was happening to these
believers, they came to see for themselves, just

what was going on. They were amazed. Why? Because what they heard was those <u>men of God speaking in their own tongue.</u> In other words, it was <u>understood by all</u> who heard what was being said in the <u>language that they spake.</u> The only power that could make this happen is the <u>Holy Spirit. God is not a God of confusion.</u>

We know that Babel or Babylon means confusion. This is amazing indeed that each person, no matter what language he spake, <u>each could understand exactly what was being said. They did not need an interpreter to tell them what was said.</u> This is the true language of the Holy Spirit as spoken by the believers on Pentecost Day. As we go on in this chapter, we will find some straight Bible teaching.

Acts 2:12-21

12. And <u>they were amazed,</u> and were in doubt, saying one to another, What meaneth this?

13. Others mocking said, <u>These men are full of new wine.</u>

14. But Peter, standing up with the eleven, lifted up his voice, and said unto them, Ye men of Judaea, and all ye that dwell at Jerusalem, be this known unto you, and hearken to my words:

15. For these are <u>not drunken,</u> as ye suppose, seeing it is but the third hour of the day.

16. But this is that which was <u>spoken by the prophet Joel:</u>

17. And it shall <u>come to pass in the last days,</u> saith God, <u>I will pour out of my Spirit upon</u>

all flesh: and your sons and your daughters shall prophesy, and your young men shall see visions, and your old men shall dream dreams:

18. And on my servants and on my handmaidens I will pour out in those days of my Spirit; and they shall prophesy:

19. And I will shew wonders in heaven above, and signs in the earth beneath; blood, and fire, and vapour of smoke:

20. The sun shall be turned into darkness, and the moon into blood, before that great and notable day of the Lord come:

21. And it shall come to pass, that whosoever shall call on the name of the Lord shall be saved. (KJV)

As we observe in verse 17, Peter in quoting from Joel, says that this will come to pass in the last days. This pouring out of the Holy Spirit was necessary at that time, to show the unbelievers at the early beginnings of the Church the power of God, through the Holy Spirit. We see further on in this chapter how thousands of souls were added to the kingdom.

Acts 2:37-42

37. Now when they heard this, they were pricked in their heart, and said unto Peter and to the rest of the apostles, Men and brethren, what shall we do?

38. Then Peter said unto them, Repent, and be baptized every one of you in the name of Jesus Christ for the remission of sins and

ye shall receive the gift of the Holy Spirit.

39. For the promise is <u>unto you, and to your children,</u> and to all <u>that are afar off, even as many as the Lord our God shall call.</u>

40. And with many other words did he testify and exhort, saying, Save yourselves from this untoward generation.

41. Then they that gladly received his word were baptized: and the same day <u>there were added unto them about three thousand souls.</u>

42. And they continued steadfastly in the apostles' doctrine and fellowship, and in breaking of bread, and in prayers. (KJV)

God then used the Holy Spirit at that time, to show his power, and to start his church or body, and put us into the Christian Age. We know that many believers will say that what was good for the Apostles then, is still good for us today. We agree, as long as it is the <u>true tongue spoken of on Pentecost day,</u> where whatever is said is <u>understood by all in there own language.</u> Now let's look at what Paul was really talking about in 1 Corinthians about speaking in tongues.

First we will look at an overview of the book to see why Paul wrote to the church at Corinth. As you examine this book, you will find that it is not a book commending them, but a book of correction. This church had a lot of problems with fornication, envy, division, and carnal ways. Paul lets them know how carnal they were, when he stated to them these passages.

1 Cor. 3:1-3

1. And I, brethren, <u>could not speak unto you as unto spiritual, but as unto carnal, even as unto babes in Christ.</u>

2. I have <u>fed you with milk,</u> and <u>not with meat:</u> for hitherto ye were <u>not able to bear it,</u> neither yet now are ye able.

3. For ye are <u>yet carnal:</u> for whereas there is <u>among you envying, and strife, and divisions, are ye not carnal, and walk as men?</u> (KJV)

Going deeper into the subject of speaking in an unknown tongue and what Paul had to say about this subject, we will look into the Greek meaning of the word *tongue.*

1100 glossa (gloce-sah');
of uncertain affinity; the tongue; by implication; <u>a language (specially, one naturally unacquired):</u>

In the Thayer's definition, we find the following meanings to this word.

1100 glossa-

1. <u>the tongue, a member of the body, an organ of speech</u>

2. <u>a tongue; the language or dialect used by a particular people</u> distinct from that of other nations

We will go into the *American Heritage Dictionary* to find the meaning of the word *naturally.*

1. <u>In a natural manner.</u>
2. By <u>nature;</u> inherently.

3.   Without a doubt; surely.

We know that the natural man cannot see or understand the things of God. Therefore in the natural, we could not speak a language or speak and be understood by all that are around us, unless it was through the Holy Spirit. Now going further into this, we read a passage in 1 Corinthians, which a lot of Christians use to justify their speaking in tongues.

1 Cor. 12:10

> 10.   To another the working of miracles; to another prophecy; to another discerning of spirits; to another divers kinds of tongues; to another the interpretation of tongues: (KJV)

These are gifts that Paul is referring to. But what does this word **another** mean? Going into the Greek, we find this meaning for the word *another.*

243 allos (al'-los);
a primary word; "else," i.e., different (in many applications):

Although the King James Version translates this as *another,* looking at this word in the Greek, it means different. So what Paul was really saying is that they were given different gifts to each believer, and not another to each person. The working of miracles needs a little mention, because the word *miracles* in the Greek has a special meaning.

1411 dunamis (doo'-nam-is);
from 1410; force (literally or figuratively); spe-

cially, miraculous power (usually by implication, a miracle itself):

This deals with God's power that all believers
have in Christ. When you receive Christ in you,
then his power is implanted in you. You as believers have this miraculous power within, to
thwart off the Devil, to pray for the sick, and to
help you in your Christian walk. We believe in
what was said about calling for the elders to lay
hands on the sick and to pray for them.

James 5:14

14. Is any sick among you? let him call for the
    elders of the   church; and let them pray
    over him, anointing him with oil in the
    name of the Lord: (KJV)

We will now go back into 1 Corinthians 12:10
and look at other meanings to these words as
spoken in Greek, which is the common language
used in the translation of the New Testament.

The word *divers* was added by the translators, and does not have any special meaning in
this or other verses concerning tongues. The
word **KIND** has a meaning that may surprise you
when you see this word in its Greek form.

1085 genos (ghen'-os);
from 1096 "kin" (abstract or concrete, literal or
figurative, individual or collective):

This is interesting, as the word **kin** means
your kinfolk or relatives. Now *Thayer's* definition
goes further into explaining this meaning.

1085 genos-
1) race

a) <u>offspring</u>
b) <u>family</u>
c) stock, race, <u>nation,</u>
d) that is, <u>nationality or descent from a par-</u>
<u>ticular people</u>
e) the aggregate of many individuals of the same nature, kind, sort

As this is so at variance with what we think that this word means, we feel that the definition of this word should be exhausted through all sources. *Vine's Expository Dictionary* has this to say for the meaning of this word:

BEGET, BEAR (OF BEGETTING), BORN
1.   Genos 1085 , "a generation, kind, stock," is used in the dative case, with the article, to signify <u>"by race,"</u> in <Acts 18:2;> and <24>, RV, for the KUV, "Born."
See **COUNTRYMEN, DIVERSITY, GENER-ATION, KIND, <u>KINDRED,</u> NATION, OFF-SPRING, STOCK**
(From *Vine's Expository Dictionary of Biblical Words*)

We went into these different meanings to show that what Paul was talking about, was not <u>diverse unknown tongues,</u> but different dialects spoken throughout the areas of Paul's teachings. The words *diverse* and *unknown* are in italics because these words were added by the translators. The word *interpretation* has this meaning in the Greek.

2058 hermeneia (her-may-ni'ah);
from the same as 2059; translation:

This puts a different light on the subject, as we see that to interpret means to translate. If you were in a church where Spanish was the language spoken, then got up during the services and spoke English, and nobody could translate your message, then your words would be in vain. In Paul's day, and in Christ's, the common practice was to pass the manuscripts around and each would take his turn reading Scriptures. Example of this is found in Luke:

Luke 4:17-20

17. <u>And there was delivered unto him the book</u> of the prophet Esaias. And when <u>he had opened the book,</u> he found the place where it was written,

18. The Spirit of the Lord is upon me, because he hath anointed me to preach the gospel to the poor; he hath send me to heal the brokenhearted, to preach deliverance to the captives, and recovering of sight to the blind, to set at liberty them that are bruised,

19. To preach the acceptable year of the Lord.

20. And he closed the book, and he gave it again to the minister, and sat down. And the eyes of all them that were in the synagogue were fastened on him. (KJV)

There were not preachers as we know them today. Each person would stand up and recite some Scriptures. And then this would be discussed among them. Because there were people coming from all parts of the country to worship, some spoke in different languages. So then if one wished to expound on Scripture in the presence of others who might not speak that tongue, an interpreter or translator was necessary, so all could understand and be edified. Let's go further into Corinthians and look at chapter 13, which is known as the lave chapter.

God's Love to Us

1 Cor. 13:4

4. <u>Charity</u> suffereth long, and is kind; charity envieth not; charity vaunteth not itself, is not puffed up, (KJV)

It is commonly believed that he was talking in general to Christians. But through further examination, we found that he was talking about God's love. Going into the original Greek writings, it is evident that a word was left out of this verse in the translation. The word before Charity (which means love) in the Greek is Hee, which is a definite article. Hee is in the third person meaning he, she, it, etc. His or God's is a definite article, so this verse should read "God's love suffereth long, and is kind; God's love envieth not, God's love vaunteth not itself, is not puffed up." Then the love chapter is about God's love to us.

We should strive to love God with all our hearts and love our neighbors as ourselves, which was Christ's commandment to us, but as <u>we are not perfect</u> creations, we fail on occasions, so we cannot say our love will not fail. How beautiful is God's love that though we were yet sinners Christ died for us (Rom. 5:8).

We will now go into chapter 14 of 1 Corinthians and see exactly what Paul said concerning tongues. In the first four verses, we read the following:

1 Cor. 14:1-4

1. <u>Follow after charity, and desire spiritual gifts, but rather that ye may prophesy.</u>

2. For he that <u>speaketh in an</u> unknown <u>tongue speaketh not unto men, but unto God for no man understandeth him;</u> howbeit <u>in the spirit he speaketh mysteries.</u>

3. But he that prophesieth speaketh unto men to edification, and exhortation, and comfort.

4. He that speaketh in an unknown tongue edifieth himself, but he that prophesieth edifieth the church. (KJV)

In verse 1, the original manuscripts concerning this passage of Scripture were written in this manner. The word *gifts* were added by the translators.

Follow after his love, desire the spiritual, also speak under inspiration.

The word *prophesy* has the meaning that we used, but we will go into *Strong's Exhaustive Concordance* to show the Greek meaning for prophesy.

4395 propheteuo (prof-ate-yoo'-o);
from 4396; to foretell events, divine, <u>speak under inspiration exer</u>cise the <u>prophetic office:</u>

Going into verse 2, Paul says that if you speak under inspiration to men, it is for their edification, and exhortation, and comfort. If you speak in a language not understood, the congregation will not know what is being said. In essence, we know that God understands all languages. In the process of correcting them, Paul was conveying that what they were speaking, if it was possible was even a mystery to God. Prophesy also means to preach. Verse 4 shows how the manuscripts read and translate the meanings.

He that speaks in his language edifieth himself, but he that prophesieth, edifieth the church.

Paul is really criticizing this practice. The Corinthians, who were doing this, that is speaking in an unknown tongue, were trying to appear to be spiritual, even though Paul explained that it was not benefiting the church, only the ego of the person who was speaking.

One of the authors was in a church that spoke in tongues and was a witness to the following. A lady stood up in the services and spoke something that he could not understand. Well, true to what people think has to happen, they presented a interpretation of what was just said. "And thou shalt not watch *I Love Lucy* on TV." It is interesting to note that most interpretations are spoken using the King James language, like ye, thou, etc. Now did this great revelation edify the body of Christ? Hardly. Even though this kind of interpretation is rare, how do we know that what is being translated is what was originally said?

Going back to Acts 2 in which what was said

was understood by all who listened. Jesus warned us about being like the Pharisees and Scribes, who love to show off their spirituality.

The point of all this is that most churches in this country today speak English. If this is the language understood by everyone in the congregation, then there is no need to speak another tongue. Remember in Acts 2 they all understood what was being said in their own language. Let's go on and read more of this chapter.

1 Cor. 14:5-9

5. I would that <u>ye all spake with tongues, but rather that ye prophesied:</u> for greater is he that prophesieth than he that speaketh with tongues, except he interpret, that the church may receive edifying.

6. Now, brethren, if I come unto you speaking with tongues, <u>what shall I profit you, except</u> I shall <u>speak to you either by revelation,</u> or by <u>knowledge,</u> or <u>by prophesying,</u> or <u>by doctrine?</u>

7. And even things <u>without life giving sound,</u> whether pipe or harp, <u>except they give a distinction in the</u> sounds, how shall it be known what is piped or harped?

8. For if the <u>trumpet</u> give an uncertain sound, <u>who shall prepare himself to the battle?</u>

9. So likewise ye, <u>except ye utter by the tongue words easy to be understood, how shall it be known what is spoken? for ye shall speak into the air.</u> (KJV)

Verse 5 states clearly that you should not

speak in a language not understood unless you have an interpreter or you can interpret. Remember to interpret means to translate. This is where you would need a translator. Being a good translator is also a gift, because if the translator can translate with the same emotion in which your message is being delivered, the audience will fully understand what you are trying to convey. Now if the interpreter only uses a monotone voice to translate your message, then the impact of how you are trying to say something is lost in the translation.

Going to verse 7 of this chapter, we find the same thing used earlier in this book when Paul uses this phrase.

1 Cor. 13:1

1. Though I speak with the <u>tongues of men and of angels,</u> and have <u>not charity,</u> I am become as sounding brass, or a tinkling cymbal. (KJV)

In the first part of the love chapter, which we covered earlier, we are going to put a part of it as it was originally written for clarity.

The same language he speaks to men, he can speak to angels.

Without God's love, everything would be as sounding brass, and tinkling cymbals. Without the Holy Spirits' guidance, in your study of God's word, most of the Bible would not be understood. For it is the Holy Spirit that discerns and gives to believers, the deep things of God.

Verse 8 tells a big story. If we do not understand the truth of God's word, and know when Antichrist is coming, and when Christ will appear, then you will not understand, or hear the trumpet. Also without fortifying yourself in the Scriptures, you will not be prepared for that great battle, with Antichrist in the end times. In the case of verse 9, it should read.

If you speak in a language, not understood, then you are talking a lot of hot air, as nobody understands what is being said.

Going on in this chapter, we find more evidence that the tongue is nothing more than a language, spoken on this earth.

1 Cor. 14:10-13

10. There are, it may be, so many kinds of <u>voices</u> in the world, and none of them is without signification_

11. Therefore if <u>I know not the meaning of the voice, I shall be unto him that speaketh a barbarian, and he that speaketh shall be a barbarian unto me.</u>

12. Even so ye, forasmuch as ye are zealous of spiritual <u>gifts, seek that ye may excel to the edifying of the church.</u>

13. Wherefore let him that <u>speaketh</u> in an unknown <u>tongue pray that</u> <u>he may interpret</u>. (KJV)

The word *voice* in the Greek is interesting, as we use this word every day.

5456 phone (fo-nay');
probably akin to 5316 through the idea of disclosure; a tone (articulate, bestial or artificial); by implication, an address (for any purpose),

saying or language:

This is where we get our word **phone** from. Note it is a saying, or language. This gets much clearer when we look up the word **barbarian.**

915 barbaros (bar'-bar-os);
of uncertain derivation; a foreigner (i.e., non-Greek):

The word **foreigner** only means someone not Greek, or not of that language, or origin. Prior to Paul's time, these territories had been conquered by Alexander the Great. The Hellenistic, or Greek, language was predominate. We know from history that the Jews resisted this language, and fought to keep Hebrew, as their own language.

When the Romans conquered this area, Greek still was the predominate language. There were, however, several who did not accept the Greek, and different languages were spoken, as evidenced in Acts chapter 2, when it says that there were Jews of many languages represented on the day of Pentecost. Paul also carried his ministry to different countries.

Paul was correcting the church at Corinth, because they were puffed up, and they were trying to show off their so- called spirituality. If you understand that this book was a letter from Paul, correcting them for their doctrine, then you will understand more of what Paul was talking about, by not exhorting them to continue. Going further into this chapter, we will get deeper into our subject.

1 Cor. 14:14-17

14. For if I pray in an unknown <u>tongue,</u> my spirit prayeth, but my <u>understanding is unfruitful.</u>

15. What is it then? I will pray with the spirit, and J will <u>pray with the</u> understanding also: I will sing with the spirit, and I will <u>sing with the understanding also.</u>

16. Else when thou shalt bless with the spirit, <u>how shall he that occupieth the room of the unlearned say Amen</u> at thy giving of thanks, <u>seeing he understandeth not what thou sayest?</u>

17. For thou verily givest thanks well, <u>but the other is not edified</u>. (KJV)

Paul says that you need understanding. How important that is. <u>If you do not understand what you are saying,</u> or what <u>someone else is saying,</u> how can your spirit be edified. For if the Holy Spirit, itself, does not understand what you are saying, then how can the Holy Spirit edify your Spirit?

Looking at verse 16, the word *occupied* simply means to occupy. Now the word *unlearned,* in the Greek, means this:

2399 idiotes (id-ee-o'tace);
from 2398; <u>a private person,</u> i.e.,
(by implication) <u>an ignoramus (compare "idiot"):</u>

Here is a private person, which simply put is a person who has not yet accepted Christ. If this person does not share the Christian beliefs, concerning the faith, they cannot help being confused, by not understanding what they hear.

How can they believe in the message concerning Christ? Continuing in this chapter to go deeper into the tongues of Paul's day:

1 Cor. 14:18-20

18. I thank my God, I <u>speak</u> with <u>tongues</u> more than ye all:

19. Yet in the church I had rather speak <u>five words with my understanding,</u> that by my voice J might <u>teach others</u> also, than ten thousand words in an unknown tongue.

20. Brethren, <u>be not children in understanding:</u> howbeit in malice be ye children, but <u>in understanding be men</u>. (KJV)

Paul was an educated man. He had been a Pharisee. He was well- schooled in different languages. Having this background, he could tell them that he could speak with more languages than they. In verse 18 in the original manuscripts, it reads like this:

Thanks to God, I speak more languages than you all.

He goes on to say in verse 19 that he would rather speak five words of understanding than ten thousand in another language. Paul then chastises them, getting them <u>not to be children of understanding,</u> but to <u>understand like men.</u> Getting back into this chapter of correction from Paul to the Corinthians, we read the following:

1 Cor. 14:21-25

21. In the law it is written, With <u>men of other tongues</u> and <u>other lips</u> will I <u>speak unto this people;</u> and yet for all that will they

not hear me, saith the Lord.

22. Wherefore <u>tongues are for a sign, not to them that believe, but to them that believe not:</u> but prophesying serveth not for them that believe not, but for them which believe.

23. If therefore the whole church become together into one place, and all speak with tongues, and there come in those that are unlearned, or unbelievers, will they not say that ye are mad?

24. But if all prophesy, and there come in one that believeth not, or one unlearned, he is convinced of all, he is Iudged of all:

25. And thus are the secrets of his heart made manifest; and so falling down on his face he will worship God, and report that God is in you of a truth. (KJV)

Verse 21 was quoted from Isaiah, which we will also put into this chapter.

Isa. 28:11

1. For with <u>stammering</u> lips and another tongue will he speak to this people. (KJV)

The word <u>stammering</u> in Isaiah has this meaning in the Hebrew.

3934 la' eg (law-ayg');
from 3932; a buffoon; also a <u>foreigner:</u>

In the Greek <u>with other</u> has this meaning:

2084 heteroglossos (het-er-og'-loce-sos);
from 2087 and 1100; <u>othertongued, i.e., a for-</u>

eigner:

We see that both languages basically mean the same thing, a foreign language. In essence, Paul was saying that other peoples, of other languages, will talk to God's people. Today we have English, which was not heard of in Paul's time. There are also believers, in many parts of the world, today speaking different languages, and God is still speaking to his people.

Here now is the main point of this subject. In verse 22, Paul goes on to say that tongues are for a sign, not to them that believe, but to them that believe not. Refer back to Acts chapter 2, where they all heard the word, in their own tongues, even though the speakers were from Galilee, speaking in their own language. This was a sign to those who did not believe. Verse 23 verifies what the authors have seen in their own experiences. If an unbeliever or unlearned in Scripture comes into a church, and there are people speaking in tongues, they will think they are mad and leave. If all there is to the language is babel, or confusion, and not the true language, of the Holy Spirit, then an outsider, or even someone in the church, will think they are crazy.

As verse 24 and 25 says, when you come together, and speak the inspired word in understanding, then he will be convinced, and judged of all. Hearing the truth will bring sinners to repentance, and not confusion. Next we read that Paul says all things in the church should be in order.

1 Cor. 14:26-33

26. How is it then, brethren? when ye collie

together, every one of you hath a psalm, hath a doctrine, hath a <u>tongue,</u> hath a revelation, hath an <u>interpretation.</u> Let all things be done <u>unto edifying.</u>

27. If any man speak in an unknown <u>tongue, let it be by two, or at the</u> most <u>by three,</u> and that by course; and <u>let one interpret.</u>

28. But if there be <u>no interpreter, let him keep silence in the church; and let him speak to himself, and to God.</u>

29. Let the <u>prophets speak two or three,</u> and let the <u>other judge.</u>

30. If any thing be revealed to another that sitteth by, let the first hold his peace.

31. For ye may all prophesy one by one, that all may learn, and all may be comforted.

32. And the spirits of the prophets are subject to the prophets.

33. For <u>God is not the author of confusion,</u> but of peace, as in all churches of the saints. (KJV)

As we have stated before, in these churches of Paul's time, there were no pastors as we know them today. Christians would get up and read Scripture or talk about their doctrines. After they were through, then it would be discussed among the congregation. With this in mind, verse 27 then makes sense, when it reads, that if there are people among them who speak other languages, let them speak in twos or threes, and have someone to interpret. If no one is there to interpret, then let those persons keep silent, and speak to themselves and to God.

Verse 33 sums it all up when Paul declares, "God is not the author of confusion, but of peace." So all things in the church should be done in an orderly fashion, so the Saints can be edified. This is amplified in the following verses:

1 Cor. 14:37-40

37. If any man think himself to be a <u>prophet, or spiritual,</u> let him acknowledge that the things that I write unto you are the <u>commandments of the Lord.</u>

38. <u>But if any man be ignorant, let him be ignorant.</u>

39. Wherefore, brethren, <u>covet to prophesy,</u> and <u>forbid not to speak with tongues.</u>

40. Let all things be done decently and in order. (KJV)

Paul says that what he wrote was a commandment of the Lord. The authors cannot emphasize more, as to what is said then in verse 38. This speaks for itself. Verse 39 has been used by evangelicals, to substantiate their speaking in an unknown tongue. All Paul was referring to back then was if a person does not speak in your language, do not deny them the right to worship with you, providing that when they speak it can be understood by all, through a translator. Paul understood this concept. This is why he said; do not forbid those who speak in a different tongue from you to speak.

Remember, this was a letter of correction for the Corinthians, to set them back on track. We know that God is not a respecter of persons. He looks on us all as his creation. We therefore should do the same. In Paul's last statement, he proclaims that everything should be done decently and orderly. It is interesting to note that only the Corinthians were plagued by the tongues problem, and Paul had to spend a lot of time explaining to them what was the correct use of language, especially the one spoken through the Holy Spirit, so everyone can understand what is being said. This is not what some of today's traditions seem to imply. We do have confusion in some of our churches. Hopefully by studying God's Word, the church will look more closely at this tradition.

The Lord's Supper

The last tradition we want to explore in this chapter is that of the Lord's Supper, or communion. Row many times has it been said in churches before the body of Christ partakes in communion, to examine yourself before you partake. The reason for this supposedly is to look for sin in your life. It has been said that if you find a sin and it is not forgiven, then you should not partake of communion. This frightens a lot of people not to partake, because they feel they missed a sin and should not participate. This confusion comes out of Paul's letter to the Corinthians, which as noted earlier was a letter of correction. Let's see exactly what Paul had to say on this subject.

20.   When ye come together therefore into one place, <u>this is not to eat the Lord's supper.</u>

21.   For in eating every one taketh before other his <u>own supper:</u> and <u>one is hungry, and another is drunken.</u>

22.   What? have ye not <u>houses to eat and to drink in?</u> or despise ye the church of God, and shame them that have not? What shall I say to you? shall I praise you in this? <u>I praise you not.</u>

23.   For I have received of the Lord that which also I delivered unto you, That the Lord Jesus the same night in which he was betrayed took bread:

24.   And when he had given thanks, he brake it, and said, Take eat: this is my body, which is broken for you: <u>this do in remembrance of me.</u>

25.   And the same manner also he took the cup, when he had supped, saying, This cup is the new testament in my blood: this do ye, as oft as ye drink it, <u>in remembrance of me.</u>

26.   For as often as ye eat this bread, and drink this cup, ye do <u>shew the Lord's death till he come.</u>

27.   Wherefore whosoever shall eat this bread, and drink this cup of the Lord, <u>unworthily,</u> shall be guilty of the body and blood of the Lord.

28.   But let a man <u>examine himself,</u> and so let

him eat of that bread, and drink of that cup.

29.   For he that eateth and drinketh <u>unworthily,</u> eateth and drinketh damnation to himself, <u>not discerning the Lord's body.</u>

30.   <u>For this cause many are weak and sickly among you, and many sleep.</u>

31.   <u>For if we would judge ourselves, we should not be judged.</u>

32.   But when <u>we are judged,</u> we <u>are chastened of the Lord,</u> that we should <u>not be condemned with the world.</u>

33.   Wherefore, my brethren, when ye come together to eat, tarry one for another.

34.   And if any man hunger, let him eat at home; that ye come not together unto condemnation. And the rest will I set in order when I come. (KJV)

What was happening to the Corinthians was that they were combining the Agape, or Love Feast, with the Lord's Supper. They would dress up in their finest clothes, and have the best they could eat, to show off to all how well their riches were. In the process of all this, the poor would be delegated the worst seats in the church, and if they had little or nothing to eat, they did without. This was a disgrace to our Lord who took his supper on the eve of his death on the cross.

Paul really chastises them, when he asked them if they didn't have houses to eat in and not in the church. They also got drunk while celebrating this feast. Paul went on to explain exactly why we celebrated this communion together. He taught them the true meaning of the Lord's Supper. Perceiving their state of mind during this feast, he clearly stated that you should enter into this knowing what you are doing. In verse 27 he declared that "whosoever shall eat this bread, and drink this cup of the Lord <u>unworthily.</u>" This is a different meaning from unworthy. We are all not worthy except that we are covered by the blood of Christ, which makes us worthy. The word **un-worthily** has the following meaning

371 anaxios (an-ax-ee'oce);

adverb from 370; <u>irreverently:</u>

In other words if you are not observing what the true meaning of our Lord's Supper, and are not reverent to Christ and his death on the cross, then you should not partake of his communion. This is a sacred event, and by taking the communion, we recognize the fact of his death for our sins. That we might possibly have sinned is not a reason for not partaking of communion. We should all seek forgiveness each day, as we are all sinners saved by grace, and will have this two natured- being in us until we shed this mortal body and take on our Spiritual body.

Going on in this chapter, verse 28 states that "a man should examine himself." Of course we should examine our frame of mind to see if we are truly "showing the Lords death until he comes." We know that it is written,

All have sinned and come short of the glory of God (Rom. 3.23).

Then our examination is to test and see if we

are in a reverent state of mind and discerning the Lord's body. No one should lay unnecessary guilt trips on the body of Christ. Paul declared that God is a God of peace. To reiterate what was said in an earlier chapter, "You make void the Word of God, by your traditions." We can also emphatically state that we feel the Holy Spirit's guidance in what is written in this book.

In the next chapter, we will go into a subject not generally taught in the church today, which is the two witnesses. We hope we have given the readers something to think about and lead them into the Word of God to study more of what God says and not men.

8

The Two Witnesses,
the Candlesticks, and
the Parable of the Fig Tree

Here we are going to be dealing with the two witnesses in Revelation. Very little is known or spoken about the two witnesses in the Book of Revelation 11:3-12. Why? Who are they? Some think that they are Elijah and Enoch because they were translated and did not see physical death. Others think that they are Elijah and Moses, since they were with Jesus when he was transfigured. You draw your own conclusions. Is there anything written about them in the Old Testament? Well, the answer is yes. In Zechariah we read the following.

Zech. 4:1-4

1. And the angel that talked with me came again, and waked me, as a man that is wakened out of his sleep,

2. And said unto me, What seest thou? And I said, I have looked, and behold a <u>candlestick</u> all of gold, with a bowl upon the top of it, and his <u>seven lamps</u> thereon, and seven pipes to the seven lamps, which are upon the top thereof:

3. And <u>two olive trees</u> by it, one upon the right side of the bowl, and the other upon the left side thereof.

4. So I answered and spake to the angel that

talked with me, saying, What are these, my lord? (KJV)

Here the prophet Zechariah only sees one golden candlestick, which is a figure of speech for the body of Christ. It is called a menorah, which is symbolic of the tree of life. We also see seven lamps and seven pipes, with a bowl on its top. Notice that there are two olive trees. One on the right, and one on the left side of the bowl. What is this candlestick with the seven lamps and two olive trees? To further look into this mystery, we will go to Revelation and see if we can clarify some of this prophecy.

Mystery of the Meaning of the Candlesticks and the Olive Trees

Rev. 1:12-13

12. And I turned to see the voice that spake with me. And being turned, I saw <u>seven golden candlesticks;</u>

13. And in the midst of the seven candlesticks one like unto the Son of man, clothed with a garment down to the foot, and girt about the paps with a golden girdle. (KJV)

It is our belief that the seven candlesticks are the seven churches, which we wrote about in a previous chapter.

Rev. 1:20

20. The <u>mystery of the seven stars</u> which thou sawest in my right hand, and the <u>seven golden candlesticks.</u> The <u>seven stars are the angels</u> of the <u>seven churches:</u> and the

seven candlesticks which thou sawest are the seven churches. (KJV)

Two Olive Trees Are the Two Witnesses

This ties in with what Zechariah saw in his vision. Of course in verse 13 we see Christ is in the midst of these seven candlesticks. He is the head of the Church. Now going on into Revelation, we read the following account of the two witnesses:

Rev. 11:1-12

1. And there was given me a reed like unto a rod: and the angel stood, saying, Rise, and measure the temple of God, and the altar, and them that worship therein.

2. But the court which is without the temple leave out, and measure it not; for it is given unto the Gentiles: and the holy city shall they tread under foot forty and two months.

3. And I will give power unto my two witnesses, and they shall prophesy a thousand two hundred and threescore days, clothed in sackcloth.

4. These are the two olive trees, and the two candlesticks standing before the God of the earth.

5. And if any man will hurt them, fire proceedeth out of their mouth, and devoureth their enemies: and if any man will hurt them, he must in this manner be killed.

6. These have power to shut heaven, that it

rain not in the days of their prophecy: and have power over waters to turn them to blood, and to smite the earth with all plagues, as often as they will.

7.　And when they shall have <u>finished their testimony, the beast that ascendeth out of the bottomless pit shall make war against them, and shall overcome them, and kill them.</u>

8.　And their dead bodies shall lie in the street of the great city, which spiritually is called Sodom and Egypt, where also our Lord was crucified.

9.　And they of the people and kindreds and tongues and nations shall see their dead bodies three days and a half, and shall not suffer their dead bodies to be put in graves.

10.　And they that dwell upon the earth shall rejoice over them, and make merry, and shall send gifts cone to another; because these two prophets tormented them that dwelt on the earth.

11.　And <u>after three days and an half</u> the Spirit of life from God entered into them, and they stood upon their feet; and great fear fell upon them which saw them.

12.　12 And they heard a great voice from heaven saying unto them. Come up hither. And they <u>ascended up to heaven in a cloud;</u> and their enemies beheld them. (KJV)

Looking at verse 3, we find the two witnesses

clothed in sackcloth, which is symbolic of mourning. These witnesses will be in a state of mourning as they are trying to teach the church the truth, that Satan is Antichrist and not the real Messiah. In verse 4 we only see two candlesticks are with the two witnesses. Verse 7 is something that should be considered by the Body of Christ, in that it clearly states that the two witnesses prophesy <u>before</u> the coming of Antichrist to give the truth to those who will listen.

Seven Lamps and Two Candlesticks

We would like to draw to the attention of the readers that Zechariah saw one candlestick with seven lamps and two olive trees, while in Revelation it only mentions two olive trees with two candlesticks. Does this really contradict what Zechariah saw? No! Because the two candlesticks are the two churches, written in Rev. 2:8-10 and Rev. 3:7-21.

In addition when you understand the parable of the ten virgins, it is written that they all had lamps, so when you add the five virgins along with the two candlesticks written in Revelation, what Zechariah saw would be correct, being one candlestick with seven lamps. We would also like to amplify the fact that Zechariah saw <u>seven lamps,</u> not <u>candlesticks.</u> Now let's look at these two churches written about in Revelation.

Rev. 2:8-11

8. And unto the angel of the church in Smyrna write, These things saith the first and the last, which was dead, and is alive;

9. I know thy works, and tribulation, and poverty, (but thou art rich) and I <u>know the blasphemy of them which say they are Jews, and are not, but are the synagogue of Satan.</u>

10. <u>Fear none of those things which thou shalt suffer:</u> behold, the devil shall cast some of you into prison, that ye may be tried, and <u>ye shall have tribulation ten days:</u> be thou faithful unto death, and I will give thee a crown of life.

11. He that hath an ear, let him hear what the Spirit saith unto the churches. He that overcometh shall not be hurt of the second death. (KJV)

What we have is here Christ held nothing against this church. Now going on to the next church, we read the following:

Rev. 3:7-13

7. And to the angel of the church in Philadelphia write; These things saith he that is holy, he that is true, he that hath the key of David, he that openeth, and no man shutteth; and shutteth, and no man openeth;

8. I know thy works: behold, I have set before thee an open door, and no man can shut it: for thou hast a little strength, and hast kept my word, and hast not denied my name.

9. Behold, I will make them of the synagogue of Satan, which say they are Jews, and are

not, but do lie; behold, I will make them to come and worship before thy feet, and to know that I have loved thee.

10. Because thou hast kept the word of my patience, I also will keep thee from the hour of temptation, which shall come upon all the world, to try them that dwell upon the earth.

11. Behold, I come quickly: hold that fast which thou hast, that no man take thy crown.

12. Him that overcometh will I make a pillar in the temple of my God, and he shall go no more out: and I will write upon him the name of my God, and the name of the city of my God, which is new Jerusalem, which cometh down out of heaven from my God: and I will write upon him my new name..

13. He that hath an ear, let him hear what the Spirit saith unto the churches. (KJV)

We also see that Christ protects these churches because of their faithfulness, so what is the common ground that binds these churches together, and sets them apart from the five other churches? The answer lies in verse 9 of both of these passages. This is why we have put double emphasis on these, because these churches knew that Satan is on earth, and setting in the seat in the temple, which should be Christ's, posing as Christ, with his children, the Kenites, who pose as the Jews. Please read 2 Thessalonians 2:3- 4. Therefore we believe that there is no contradiction between Revelation 11:4 and Zechariah's version of seven candlesticks. Refer to chapter 7 on the other five churches. Continuing on in Zechariah 4:

The Great Tribulation and the Delivering Up of the Saints

Zech. 4:5-6

5.　Then the angel that talked with me answered and said unto me, Knowest thou not what these be? And I said, No, my lord.

6.　Then he answered the spake unto me, saying, This is the word of the LORD unto <u>Zerubbabel,</u> saying, <u>Not by might, nor by power, but by my spirit, saith the LORD of hosts.</u> (KJV)

Let's look at the meaning of *Zerubbabel* and see if we can get a better idea of what is meant here.

2216 Zerubbabel (zer-oob-baw-bel');
from 2215 and 894; <u>descended of</u> (i.e., from) <u>Babylon,</u> i.e., from) Babylon, i.e., <u>born there;</u> Zerubbabel, an Israelite:

What we will now do is to use both root meanings to extract a bigger picture of what we are writing about.

2215 zarab (zaw-rab');
a primitive root; <u>to flow away;</u> KJV—wax warm.

The other root word has this meaning:

894 Babel <u>(baw-bel');</u>

from J101; <u>confusion; Babel</u> (i.e., Babylon), including Babylonia and the Babylonian <u>empire</u>:

To exhaust this word, which will help us to fully understand where we are going with this, let's see what we can find out.

1101 balal (baw-lal');
a primitive root; <u>to overflow (specifically with oil);</u> by implication, to <u>mix;</u>
also (denominatively from 1098) <u>to fodder:</u>

Looking at these meanings, we can link them to other prophecies, even those spoken by Christ himself in Matthew. From the meanings of *mix* and *fodder,* we can see why Jesus talked about false prophets coming in to deceive many. They will mix in with God's people and feed them traditions not backed by Scripture, which is what Satan and his offspring do very well.

Matt. 24:11-13

11. And <u>many false prophets shall rise, and shall deceive many.</u>

12. And because iniquity shall abound, the love of many shall <u>wax cold.</u>

13. But he that shall endure unto the end, the same shall be saved. (KJV)

This coincides also with Revelation concerning Babylon or confusion in John's revelation to the Body of Christ.

Rev. 18:4-5

And I heard another voice from heaven, saying, <u>Come out of her, my people,</u> that ye <u>be not partakers of her sins,</u> and that ye <u>receive</u>

not of her plagues.

5 For her sins have reached unto heaven, and God hath remembered her iniquities.(KJV)

As stated before, how can you come out of something, unless you are already in there? You have to be in this confusion or one- world system during the Great Tribulation, to be able to come out of it. Then the Body of Christ will not be a partaker of Satan's sins, or the plagues, which will be sent on Antichrist and his servants. We know that the Church is in the Great Tribulation because Christ states this in Matthew.

Matt. 24:22

22. And except those days should be shortened, there should no flesh be saved: but for the elect's sake those days shall be shortened. (KJV)

In Revelation, the time frame is identified as to how long these days have been shortened.

Rev. 9:10-11

10. And they had tails like unto scorpions, and there were stings in their tails; and their power was to hurt men five months.

11. And they had a king over them, which is the angel of the bottomless pit, whose name in the Hebrew tongue is Abaddon, but in the Greek tongue hath his name Apollyon. (KJV)

We see that men can be hurt only five months. The word **hurt** has a different meaning when you look at it in the Greek.

91 adikeo (ad-ee-keh'-o);
from 94; <u>to be unjust,</u> i.e., (actively) <u>do wrong</u>
<u>(morally, socially,</u> or <u>physically):</u>

So then we are not talking about a physical hurt, but a spiritual hurt, as they are unjust and do morally wrong for five months. The king over them is none other than Satan himself as we look to the meaning of Apollyon in the Greek.

623 Apolluon (ap-ol-loo'-ohn);
active participle of 622; a <u>destroyer (i.e., Satan):</u>

We now see that the destroyer, Satan, will be on the scene five months. In the parable of the fig tree, it says that when you see these things that are near, even at the door, it only means that Christ's coming is imminent. We feel that Christ could come in the fall or the harvest time of the year. We are not picking a date or a year, just giving the facts of what the Scriptures reveal.

So we believe that the persecution of the Great Tribulation, or the delivering up of the Saints, will be shortened to five months, according to Revelation 9:5 and 10. The word *elect* is the same as saints. This then is another confirmation that the Saints or Church will be here. More on this in our last chapter.

Going further into Zechariah we read the following.

Zech. 4:7

7.   Who art thou, <u>0 great mountain?</u> before Zerubbabel <u>thou shalt become a plain:</u> and

he shall bring forth the headstone thereof with shouting, crying, Grace, grace unto it. (KJV)

What is this mountain that Zechariah is talking about? This is nothing more than Satan's one-world government, which the Kenites, at this present time, are setting up for their father, when he comes on the scene. To give you more clarification that the previous verse is in reference to Satan and his children, let's look at the Book of Matthew again.

The Mountain and the Fig Tree, or the Devil and the Kenites and Their Government

Matt. 21:17-22

17. And he left them, and went out of the city into Bethany; and he lodged there.

18. Now in the morning as he returned into the city, he hungered.

19. And when he saw a fig tree in the way, he came to it, and found nothing thereon, but leaves only, and said unto it; Let no fruit grow on thee henceforward forever. And presently the fig tree withered away.

20. And when the disciples saw it, they marvelled, saying, How soon is the fig tree withered away!

21. Jesus answered and said unto them, Verily J say unto you, If ye have faith, and doubt

not, ye shall not only do this which is done to the fig tree, but also if ye shall say unto <u>this mountain.</u> Be thou removed, and be thou cast into the sea; it shall be done. (KJV)

What does this signify? Here in these passages of Scripture, the parallel of the fig tree, and the mountain, are being combined into one specific event. Another account of this event that shows the same correlation is found in Mark:

Mark 11:12-14

12. And on the morrow, when they were come from Bethany, he was hungry:

13. And seeing a <u>fig tree afar off having leaves,</u> he came, if haply he might find any thing thereon: and when he came to it, he found <u>nothing but leaves; for the time of figs was not yet.</u>

14. And Jesus answered and said unto it, <u>No man eat fruit of thee hereafter for ever. And his disciples heard it</u>. (KJV)

Once again in the gospel of Mark, we find the fig tree being used to demonstrate a lesson to Christ's disciples. As we go on further in the Book of Mark, we find this written:

Mark 11:20-24

20. And in the morning, as they passed by, they saw <u>the fig tree dried up</u> from the roots.

21. And Peter calling to remembrance saith unto him, Master, behold, <u>the fig tree which thou cursedst is withered away.</u>

22. And Jesus answering saith unto them, Have faith in God.

23. For verily I say unto you, That whosoever shall say unto this mountain, Be thou removed, and be thou cast into the sea; and shall not doubt in his heart, but shall believe that those things which he saith shall come to pass; he shall have whatsoever he saith.

24. Therefore I say unto you, What things so ever ye desire, when ye pray, believe that ye receive them, and ye shall have them. (KJV)

Jesus' encounter with the fig tree is in association with teaching his disciples, as to how the saints who would be living in the generation when Satan, Apollyon, is cast to the earth, and Jesus' elect as mentioned in Revelation are brought before him. Therefore Jesus was teaching his disciples, so they would record this for use by the Holy Spirit, to the Saints who will delivered up during the Great Tribulation. In Matthew chapter 24, when Jesus was referring to the stars falling from heaven, which is in verse 29, when he reaches verse 32, he makes this astounding challenge to his followers:

The Real Parable of the Fig Tree

Matt. 24:32-33

32. Now learn a parable of the fig tree; When his branch is yet tender, and putteth forth leaves, ye know that summer is nigh:

33. So likewise ye, when ye <u>shall see all these things, know that it is near, even at the doors</u>. (KJV)

Unfortunately, the majority of Christians, pastors and laymen, have been misled into believing that the nation of Israel, established in 1948, was the fulfillment of this verse of Scripture. Nothing could be further from the truth, because each reference, with the fig tree from the time of Adam and Eve, until the cursing of the fig tree by Jesus, has always carried a negative aspect to it. The true parable of the fig tree has been overlooked by most scholars. That parable is in Luke chapter 13:

Luke 13:1-10

1. There were present at that season some that told him of the Galilaeans, whose blood Pilate had mingled with their sacrifices.

2. And Jesus answering said unto them. Suppose ye that these Galilaeans were sinners above all the Galilaeans, because they suffered such things?

3. I tell you, Nay: but, except ye repent, ye shall all likewise perish.

4. Or those eighteen, upon whom the tower in Siloam fell, and slew them, think ye that they were sinners above all men that dwell in Jerusalem?

5. I tell you, Nay: but, except ye repent, ye shall all likewise perish.

6. He spake also this *parable;* A certain man

had a fig *tree* planted in his vineyard; and he came and sought fruit thereon, and found none.

7. Then said he unto the dresser of his vineyard, Behold, these three years I come seeking fruit on this fig tree, and find none: cut it down; why cumbereth it the ground?

8. And he answering said unto him, Lord, let it alone this year also, till I shall dig about it, and dung it:

9. And if it bear fruit, well: and if not, then after that thou shalt cut it down.

10. And he was teaching in one of the synagogues on the sabbath. (KJV)

In verses 1 through 5, the subject is human sacrifices. In verse 1 the meaning of <u>some</u> has this meaning:

5100 tis (tis);
<u>an enclitic</u> indefinite pronoun; some or any person or object:

We will look at the meaning of **enclitic:**

en-clit-ic (en-klit ik) *Linguistics. noun*
A word or particle that has no independent accent and forms an accentual and sometimes also graphemic unit with the preceding word. In *Give 'em the works,* the pronoun 'em is an enclitic. *adjective*
Forming an accentual unit with the preceding

word, and thus having no independent accent. **Late Latin *encliticus,* from Greek *enklitkos,* from *enklinein,* to learn:**

So what was actually taking place in verses 1 through 5, were the Kenites coming in among other people, who were responsible for the murders of these men. Jesus, knowing who they were, begins to address them in verse 2 through 5, concerning the Galileans who had been murdered, and 18 who had been killed by the tower of Siloam. Jesus asked them questions. Did these men think, because of the tragic types deaths that those people suffered, that they were worse than all the sinners? Then he said nay in verse 5 and continued, "Except you repent, you shall all likewise perish."

Then in verse 6, he actually gives the parable of the fig tree. In these verses of Scriptures, in the manuscripts, it was revealed, in verse 7, that Satan was to be taken back to heaven with Christ when he ascended and went back to heaven. We have found that these words were withheld from the King James Version and could not be found unless you had the manuscripts.

Therefore the parable of the fig tree was nothing less than Jesus telling the Kenites that God did not want them to be destroyed, but he was giving them those three years to be taught, and given the opportunity to repent, and be saved. Further documentation that the fig tree is the devil, and his angels, and the leaves, being the Kenites, is shown in Revelation chapter 6:

Rev. 6:12-13

12. And I beheld when he had opened the <u>sixth seal,</u> and, lo, there was a great earth-quake; and the sun became black as sack-cloth of hair, and the moon became as blood;

13. <u>And the stars of heaven fell unto the earth, even as a fig tree casteth her untimely figs, when she is shaken of a mighty wind</u>. (KJV)

The above passages should clearly show that the fig tree is the Devil and his angels, who will be joined with the Kenites on earth, once they have been cast down, and not the nation Israel, which if anything, would have been symbolized as an olive tree, not a fig tree.

This is all pertinent to the two witnesses as they will be here during that time to set the record straight to those who have eyes to see and ears to hear, who Satan really is, and that the Church, or Body of Christ, shall not worship Antichrist, when he appears on the scene. To continue in our study of the two witnesses, we will document that this mountain is symbolic for government, in a prophetic sense. As an example, consider Ezekiel:

Ezek. 28:16

16. By the multitude of thy merchandise they have filled the midst of thee with violence, and thou hast sinned: therefore I will <u>cast thee as profane out of the mountain of God:</u> and I will destroy thee, 0 covering cherub, from the midst of the stones of fire. (KJV)

Here was the story of Satan in his overthrow in the world that was before this earth age, when he was cast out of God's government, which here was called the mountain of God. Another example of a mountain being referred to as the seat of government is found in Micah.

Micah 4:1-2

1. But in the last days it shall come to pass, that the <u>mountain of the house of the LORD</u> shall be established in the <u>top of the mountains,</u> and it shall be exalted <u>above the hills;</u> and people shall flow unto it.

2. And many nations shall come, and say, Come, and let us go up to the <u>mountain of the LORD,</u> and to the house of the God of Jacob; and he will teach us of his ways, and we will walk in his paths: for the law shall go forth of Zion, and the word of the LORD from Jerusalem. (KJV)

These passages tell us how a mountain is used for government. When you look into verse 1, and look at the manuscripts, and the meanings of these words, it should be read thus: "the mountain of the house of the LORD will be established as the head of the mountains and shall be above the little hills." This only means that God's government will be the head of all governments during the Millennium and will be over all the little governments of this world. These are just a few examples where government is symbolic of mountains. Therefore the mountain in Zechariah 4:7 is symbolic of Babylon the Great headed by Antichrist or Satan. To show that this mountain and the fig tree are connected and are in fact one entity, we will look at what Christ said about the mountain in the Book of Mark.

Mark 11:21-24

21. And Peter calling to remembrance saith unto him, Master, <u>behold the fig tree which thou cursedst is withered away.</u>

22. And Jesus answering saith unto them, <u>Have faith in God.</u>

23. For verily I say unto you, That whosoever shall say unto <u>this mountain, Be thou removed, and be thou cast into the sea;</u> and shall <u>not doubt in his heart,</u> but <u>shall believe</u> that those things which he saith shall come to pass; he shall have whatsoever he saith.

24. Therefore I say unto you. What things soever ye desire, when ye pray, believe that ye receive them_e and ye shall have them. (KJV)

As we discussed earlier in this chapter, the fig tree being Satan as he is to be withered and cursed, so then the mountain that Christ was referring to in these verses signifies Satan's one-world government.

The Delivering Up of the Two Witnesses Along with Those Who Do Not Follow Antichrist

In the end times, the two witnesses will be

delivered up before Antichrist. Also those who do not follow Antichrist, or Satan, will also be delivered up to take their stand for God. To document this we will go into Matthew 10. Matthew 10:16- 23 reads:

16. Behold, I <u>send you forth as sheep in the midst of wolves:</u> be ye therefore wise as <u>serpents,</u> and harmless as doves.

17. But beware of men: for they will <u>deliver you up to the councils,</u> and they will scourge you in their synagogues;

18. And ye shall be <u>brought before governors and kings</u> for my sake, for a <u>testimony against them</u> and the Gentiles.

19. But when they <u>deliver you up, take no thought how or what ye shall speak: for it shall be given you in that same hour what ye shall speak.</u>

20. For it is not <u>ye that speak,</u> but <u>the Spirit of your Father</u> which speaketh in you.

21. And the <u>brother shall deliver up the brother</u> to death, and the <u>father the child: and the children shall rise up against their parents, and cause them to be put to death.</u>

22. And ye shall be <u>hated of all men for my name's sake;</u> but he that <u>endureth to the end shall be saved.</u>

23. But when they persecute you in this city, flee ye into another: for verily I say unto you, <u>Ye shall not have gone over the cities of Israel, till the Son of man be come.</u> (KJV)

Looking at verse 16, the word **serpent** has a

special meaning, and also in the original manuscripts this word was preceded by the definite article.

3789 ophis (of-is);

probably from 3700 (through the idea of sharpness of vision); a snake, figuratively (as a type of sly cunning) an artful malicious person, <u>especially Satan:</u>

So it reads to be as wise as Satan. The only way this can be done is by reading and understanding the Word of God. To be harmless as a dove also has a special meaning, as the dove signifies the Holy Spirit. Remember when Christ was baptized, the Holy Spirit came down like a dove. So to be harmless as a dove is to allow the Holy Spirit to work through you when you are delivered up to Antichrist.

Was This Really End-Time Prophecy?

This is end-time prophecy because Christ was referring to his Second Coming in verse 23. So these verses are end-time prophecy that was given to us who have eyes to see and ears to hear. Note that the day of Pentecost and the Holy Spirit had not come. Let's continue in Zechariah to see just what else this prophet saw concerning the end times and the two witnesses.

Zech. 4:10

10. For who hath despised the day of small things? For they shall rejoice, and shall see the <u>plummet</u> in the hand of Zerubbabel <u>with those seven;</u> they are the eyes of the LORD, which run to and fro through the

whole earth. (KJV)

Looking at the word *plummet,* we see an interesting meaning. There are two words that comprise the word *plummet.*

68 'eben (eh'-ben);
from the root of 1129 through the meaning to
<u>build;</u> a stone:
913 bediyl (bed-eel');
from 914; alloy (because removed by <u>smeltin</u>);
by analogy, tin:

Going further into the meaning of 913, we see the following:

914 badal (baw-dal');
a primitive root; <u>to divide</u> (in variation senses literally or figuratively, separate, distinguish, differ, select, etc.):

The word *plummet* in the dictionary means:

1. A plumb bob

2. Something that weighs down or oppresses, a burden.

To sum it all up, the two witnesses interact with the candlestick and the seven lamps. The role of the two witnesses is to set the church plumb straight in doctrine to fulfill their mission in the end times. Also to set a pure foundation, as talked about by Paul.

Rom. 15:20

20. Yea, so have I strived to preach the gospel, <u>not where Christ was named, lest I should build upon another man's foundation:</u> (KJV)

It is important that we believers fervently study the Scriptures, to build on the foundation, which is Christ. So each and every believer builds on his own foundation. The apostle Paul goes into more detail about the foundations as he writes these words:

1 Cor. 3:10-15

10. According to the grace of God which is given unto me, as a wise masterbuilder, I have laid the foundation, and another buildeth thereon. But let every man take heed how he buildeth thereupon.

11. For other foundation can no man lay than that is laid, which is Jesus Christ.

12. Now if any man build upon this foundation gold, silver, precious stones, wood, hay, stubble;

13. Every man's work shall be made manifest: for the day shall declare it, because it shall be revealed by fire; and the fire shall try every man's work of what sort it is.

14. If any man's work abide which he hath built thereupon, he shall receive a reward.

15. If any man's work shall be burned, he shall suffer loss: but he himself shall be saved, yet so as by fire. (KJV)

So the fire, as spoken of in verse 15, is also documented in Peter's writings when he speaks of the end times and how we will be tried in the fire.

1 Pet. 4:12-14

12. Beloved, think it not strange concerning the <u>fiery trial</u> which is to <u>try you,</u> as though some strange thing happened unto you.

13. But rejoice, inasmuch as ye are partakers of Christ's sufferings; that, when his glory shall be revealed, ye may be glad also with exceeding joy.

14. If ye be <u>reproached for the name of Christ, happy are ye; for the spirit of glory and of God resteth upon you: on their part he is evil spoken of, but on your part he is glorified</u>. (KJV)

To sum up this chapter, the two witnesses will teach the body of Christ who the real Messiah is and will be backed by the two churches who know who Satan really is and where his seat is. We hope that if you have any controversy with what is written, that you search the Scriptures diligently to find the answers.

9

The Rapture: What Is It and Will It Take Place?

This has been one of the most debated subjects in church history. There are many theories about when it will take place. You will not find the word *rapture* anywhere in Scripture. There are pretrib, mid- trib, and post- trib arguments. Let's look into the *American Heritage Dictionary* and see if it will tell us about its meaning.

1.   The state of <u>being transported by a lofty emotion; ecstasy.</u>

2.   Often raptures. An <u>expression of ecstatic feeling.</u> See Synonyms at ECSTASY.

3.   <u>The transporting of a person from one place to another, especially</u> <u>to heaven.</u>

The meanings listed in 1 and 2 describe just how it will be, when we who remain at the Second Coming of our Lord, will change from our physical bodies into our spiritual bodies. The authores are anxiously awaiting this glorious moment, when our Lord will come to claim his own, as spoken of in Matthew 24:31 when Christ will gather together his elect or his body together. Paul also talks about this change in 1 Corinthians.

1 Cor. 15:44

44. It is <u>sown a natural body;</u> it is <u>raised a spiritual body.</u> There is a <u>natural body,</u> and there is a <u>spiritual body.</u> (KJV)

Here we see we have two bodies. We are now

in a natural body, but will be raised in a spiritual body. What a wonderful time that will be, when we can shed this sinful natural body and take on a spiritual body. But when will this happen? What about the third meaning of rapture, which shows a transporting of a person from one place to another, especially heaven.

Will the Church Be Taken?

The common belief is that we, the church, will not be here during the Great Tribulation. This is a tradition that we feel has been promulgated by the Kenites throughout the Body of Christ. What Scriptures are used to substantiate this theory? We should not believe in theories, but only in the truth according to the word of God.

The Warning about a False Rapture

The teaching to fly, first mentioned in the Old Testament, in its proper context, was end-time prophecy, as we will see when we look at the Scriptures. It is amazing, how God looked down at man, saw what was to come, and prophesied in ancient times through his prophets to foretell things that would come.

Ezekiel saw a lot of end- time prophecies and in this particular chapter; this is a prognostication of end times. The Holy Spirit revealed to Ezekiel, that in the end times, the church would be taught that they would fly, and not go through the Great Tribulation. Let's go into this chapter and analyze what was written.

Ezek. 13:1-6

1. And the word of the LORD came unto me, saying,

2. Son of man, prophesy against the <u>prophets of Israel</u> that prophesy, and say thou unto them that <u>prophesy out of their own hearts.</u> Here ye the word of the LORD.

3. Thus saith the Lord GOD; <u>Woe unto the foolish prophets, that follow their own spirit, and have seen nothing!</u>

4. 0 Israel, thy prophets are like the <u>foxes</u> in the <u>deserts.</u>

5. <u>Ye have not gone up into the gaps, neither made up the hedge for</u> the house of Israel to stand in <u>the battle in the day of the LORD.</u>

6. They <u>have seen vanity and lying divination,</u> saying, <u>The LORD saith: and the LORD hath not sent them:</u> and they have <u>made others to hope</u> that they would confirm the word. (KJV)

To show that in its proper context, that this end- time prophecy, it was made clear in verse 5. The House of Israel is the church grafted onto the tree.

Rom. 11:17

17. And if some of the <u>branches be broken off, and thou, being a wild olive tree, wert grafted in among them,</u> and with them partakest of the root and fatness of the olive tree; (KJV)

Paul was talking to non- Judeans, who also

are called Gentiles. They were grafted onto the tree. This is the Church or the body of Christ that the prophet is referring to. Now going into these Scriptures, we find in verse 3, that the prophets or ministers not preaching the Word of the Lord, but from their own hearts, or better yet, their emotions. The problem we have in the churches, which are the denominations of a particular group, is that the doctrine is set up by the leaders of that particular group, and all the ministers in this group teach what the leaders use as the doctrine of that particular denomination. Any deviation could result in their dismissal from their specific denomination. Therefore most doctrines are done by men, and usually not according to the Word of God. This is what Ezekiel was told by God in these Scriptures. They were not using the Word, but their feelings, or their minds. Going on into verse 4, this gets more interesting as the words **fox** and **desert** have the following meanings.

The following meaning for *fox is:*

7776 shu' al (shoo-awl');
or shu' al (shoo- awl'); from the same as 8168; a jackal <u>(as a burrower)</u>:

Going to the prime root of this word, we find there is more here than meets the eye.

8168 sho' al (sho'-al);
from an unused root meaning to hollow out; the palm; by extension, a handful:

This then means that there are a handful of foxes or burrowing animals, which is only a figure of speech for these prophets who are teaching the church to follow this doctrine. We can go back to the Kenites, who have crept in, and are now giving the church false doctrine. Going on with these meanings, we find the following.

2723 chorbah (khor-baw');
feminine of 2721; properly, <u>drought,</u> i.e., (by implication) a <u>desolation:</u>

This is the word for *desert.* This brings to mind the prophecy of Amos.

Amos 8:11

11. Behold, the <u>days come,</u> saith the Lord God, that I will <u>send a famine</u> in the land, <u>not a famine of bread, nor a thirst of for water, but of hearing the words of the LORD:</u>

Here the prophet Amos is talking about end times, a famine for the word of God. This is exactly what Ezekiel is saying in his end-time prophecy. Going on into verse 5, this will show exactly what is happening in the churches today.

The word **gaps** have the following meanings:

6556 perets (peh'-rets);
from 6555; a <u>break</u> (literally or figuratively): Taking this word to its prime meaning gives us a better insight.
6555 parats (paw-rats');
a primitive root; <u>to break out</u> (in many applications, direct and indirect, literal and figurative):

To put it in easy terms, the church has not broken from its traditions to show the people the truth of God's word. The word *hedge* simply means to put a wall, or a fence around them. This only means that the Body of Christ needs a hedge around it, to stand in the <u>battle in the day of the Lord.</u> This clarifies that this is absolutely an end- time prophecy. <u>The day of the Lord is Christ's second coming.</u> This is used many times in Scripture to denote the end times. Here are a few references that pertain to this subject. (Isa. 2:12, Isa. 13:6- 9, Jer. 46:10, Joel 2:31). Then this is end- time prophecy, pertaining to the Body of Christ. In verse 6, it speaks of using lying divination, which are false words or doctrine to deceive the body of Christ. What is this false word? Let's look into the meaning of <u>confirm</u> in the Hebrew and see if we can't get an insight.

6965 quwm (koom);
a primitive root; <u>to rise</u> (in various applications, literal, figurative, intensive and causative):

This means to rise or arise. Then when the prophets tell the Church in the end times that they will rise and not be here during the Great Tribulation, this is false teaching.

Verse 7 says that they have vain visions. The word *vain* has an interesting meaning in Hebrew.

7723 shay' (shawv);
or shay (shay); from the same as 7722 <u>in the sense of desolating; evil</u> (as <u>destructive),</u> literally (ruin) or <u>morally (especially guile); figuratively idolatry (as false,</u> subjective), uselessness (as <u>deceptive,</u> objective; also adverbially, in <u>vain):</u>

So the prophets in the end times are teaching a lie, and are not preparing the body, for the coming of the Lord on his day. This whole chapter deals with the prophets not telling the truth, saying that the Lord said, but he did not say. Skipping down to the meat of this chapter, we read the following:

Ezek. 13:9

9.   And mine hand shall be upon the <u>prophets that see vanity,</u> and <u>that divine lies: they shall not be in the assembly of my people,</u> neither shall they be written in the writing of the house of Israel, neither shall they enter into the land of Israel, and ye shall know that I am the Lord GOD. (KJV)

Christ said it best in Matthew about those who think they are doing God's will but have been misled because they did not learn the truth of God's word.

Matt. 7:22-23

22.   Many will <u>say to me in that day, Lord, Lord,</u> have we not <u>prophesied in thy name?</u> and in thy name <u>cast out devils? and in thy name done many wonderful works?</u>

23.   And then will I profess unto them, <u>I never knew you: depart from me, ye that work iniquity</u>. (KJV)

This may sound like strong language. It is intended to be, for this is a serious matter, when those of the Body of Christ do not check out the truth if God's word, but rely on their traditions, of what should be, not what really is. We end Ezekiel with God spelling out exactly what the lie is, and how he will treat the false prophets who divine this lie.

16. To wit, the prophets of Israel which prophesy concerning <u>Jerusalem,</u> and which see <u>visions of peace</u> for her, and there is no peace, saith the Lord GOD.

17. Likewise, thou son of man, set thy face against the <u>daughters</u> of thy people, which prophesy out of their own heart; and prophesy thou against them,

18. And say, Thus saith the Lord GOD; Woe to the women that sew pillows to all arm-holes, and make kerchiefs upon the head of every stature to hunt souls! Will ye hunt the souls of my people, and will ye save the souls alive that come unto you?

19. And will ye pollute me among my people for handfuls of barley and for pieces of bread, to slay the souls that should not die, and to save the souls alive that should not live, by your lying to my people that hear your lies?

20. Wherefore thus saith the Lord GOD; Behold, I am against your pillows, wherewith ye there hunt <u>the souls to make them fly,</u> and I will tear them from your arms, and will let the souls go, even the souls that ye hunt to <u>make them fly.</u>

These verses show how the Rapture is a secret veil, to cover up the truth, that we will be here during the Great Tribulation.

In verse 16 the words *to wit* were added by the translators and have no meaning. When we get to the prophets of Israel or the teachers to the church, the word *Jerusalem* means peace. In the Brown, Driver and Briggs definition, we can break this down into its purest form.

3389 Yeruwshalaim rarely Yeruwshalayim-
Jerusalem = "teaching of peace";
the chief city of Palestine and capital of the united kingdom and the nation of Judah after the split

Here is the teaching of peace_ This is what the Rapture theory is all about. It tells the Saints that they will not be here during the Great Tribulation, and so do not worry what Revelation has to say about the time when Satan is on earth, because we will not be here. It seems that they either cannot understand what is written, or refuse to believe what is there. A prime example is found in this part of Revelation.

Rev. 13:7

7.   And it was given unto him to make war with the saints, and to overcome them: and power was given him over all kindreds, and tongues, and nations. (KJV)

Does this look like the Saints will be gone during Antichrist's reign on earth? Isn't the Body of Christ called his Saints? Here is one example where Paul calls the Church the saints (Rom 12:13). Antichrist then will be allowed by God to overcome the Saints, during the Great Tribulation, and there will be no peace until Christ comes for his Saints, which is the good news, that in Christ we will overcome and go on to eternal life with him. If we have to lay down our lives for the name of Jesus Christ, then our reward in heaven will be even greater.

In verse 17 when it says "set thy face against," this is nothing more than condemnation of what is being taught. The word **daughters** is only a figure of speech for the brides of Christ. Verses 18 and 19 are very powerful because they condemn the lie, which is in verse 20. But let's look into verse 18 and see if we can find out what is really being said in this verse. The word <u>sew</u> can have different meanings. According to the *American Heritage Dictionary,* we read the following meanings.

1. To <u>complete successfully:</u> Our team has sewn up the championship.

2. <u>To gain complete control of; monopolize.</u>

When we look at the word **pillow,** we will see how this has been covered up by the Kenites in translation.

3704 keceth (keh'-seth);
from 3680; a cushion or pillow (as <u>covering a seat or bed):</u>

If we go into the Browns, Driver, and Briggs definition, this becomes a little clearer.

3704 keceth-
band, fillet, covered amulets, false phylacteries; <u>used by false prophetesses</u> in Israel to <u>support their demonic fortune- telling schemes</u>

Going into the prime root of this word, it all becomes enlightening.

3680 kacah (kaw-saw');
a primitive root; properly, to plump, i.e., fill up

hollows; by implication, to <u>cover</u> (for clothing or <u>secrecy):</u>

Here is a little different aspect to this meaning. Going into the Brown, Driver and Briggs definition, they define it a little better:

3680 kacah-
<u>to cover, to conceal, to hide</u>
a) (Qal) conceal, covered (participle)

What we see here is a hidden doctrine, which is sewn or woven into our lives, of an untrue doctrine. The word **pillow** means a veil. All this breaks down to a veiled truth, which is being hidden from the church, that you will have to be ready to stand in the day of Lord, when he comes the second time. There are no short cuts or easy ways out. Looking at the word **armholes** <u>we</u> have two meanings associated with this word.

679 'atstsiyl (ats-tseel');
from 680 (in its primary sense of uniting); a <u>joint of the hand (i.e., knuckle);</u>
also (according to some) a <u>party- wall</u> (Ezek. 41:8):

The other word attached to armholes has the following meaning.

3027 yad (yawd);
a primitive word; a hand (the open one [<u>indicating power, means, direction,</u> etc.], in distinction from 3709, the closed one); used (as noun, adverb, etc.) in a great variety of applications, both literally and figuratively, both proximate and remote [as follows]:

Looking into the dictionary, we find that the

word *party-wall* means, "a wall built on a boundary line of adjoining properties, shared by both owners." How interesting is this meaning, when you look at the analogy given here.

We as the church are Christ's. Satan is trying to divide the body of Christ by putting a wall between Christ and his people, using false doctrine to divide them from their rightful owner. If the Church believes that it will be raptured out of this earth before the Great Tribulation, then when Satan comes on the scene as Antichrist, some of the Body of Christ will fall into bed with Satan.

The Meat of This Chapter

Digging deeper into Ezekiel, we see just the whole message that God is giving as through his prophet.

Ezek. 13:19

19. And will ye <u>pollute me</u> among my people for <u>handfuls of barley</u> and for <u>pieces of bread,</u> to <u>slay the souls</u> that <u>should not</u> die, and to save the souls alive that should not live, by your <u>lying to my people that hear your lies</u>? (KJV)

Our Father is saying that these ministers are taking money from His people, to foment this lie. They say that they are saving souls, but in reality, it is to death, because what is Satan if he is not death? This could result in the losing of your eternal life with Christ.

The Fourth Beast and Seal of Daniel and Revelation

In Daniel's fourth beast, Satan's government is referred to as the Dreadful and Terrible Beast, and he is called the Little Horn. Now in Revelation 6:7- 8, the Devil is called death, and his government is referred to as Hell.

Dan. 7:7-8

7. After this I saw in the night visions, and behold a <u>fourth beast, dreadful and terrible,</u> and strong exceedingly; and it had great iron teeth: <u>it devoured and brake in pieces,</u> and stamped the residue with the feet of it: and it was diverse from all the beasts that were before it; and it had <u>ten horns.</u>

8. I considered the horns, and, behold, there came up among them another little horn, before whom there were three of the first horns plucked up by the roots: and, behold, in this horn were eyes like the <u>eyes of man, and a mouth speaking great things</u>. (KJV)

Rev. 6:7-8

7. And when he had opened the <u>fourth seal,</u> I heard the voice of the <u>fourth beast</u> say, Come and see.

8. And I looked and behold a <u>pale horse: and his name that sat on him was Death, and Hell followed with him.</u> And power was given unto them over the fourth part of the earth, to <u>kill with sword, and with</u>

hunger, and with death, and with the beasts of the earth. (KJV)

The Teaching to Fly

Verse 20 tells what the real lie is and what this chapter is all about. Looking into this verse, it should read like this.

Ezek. 13:20

> 20. Wherefore thus saith the Lord GOD; Behold, I am <u>against your pillows,</u> wherewith ye there hunt the <u>souls to make them fly,</u> and I will tear them from your arms, and will let the souls go, even the <u>souls that ye hunt to make them fly</u>. (KJV)

The word *fly* has the following meaning:

6524 parach (paw-rakh');
a primitive root; <u>to break forth as a bud, i.e., bloom; generally, to spread;</u>
<u>specifically, to fly (as extending the winds);</u>
figuratively, to flourish:

This is exactly what God hates, for his people to be taught that they are going to fly, or spread their wings, and leave this earth. Again we say that the Body of Christ is not being prepared to stand in the battle of the day of the Lord.

New Testament Teachings on the End Times: 1 Thessalonians

Now we will go into the New Testament, to see just what are some of the arguments that are used by some teachers today to justify this Rapture theory. The verses in 1 Thessalonians chapter 4 are some of the most prominent Scripture used to spread this theory to the Church. Verses 1-12: Paul gave the Thessalonians counsel for growth in their lives. In verses 12-18, Paul changes the subject to <u>where the dead are,</u> and why we should not grieve like the non-believers do. Let's look at these verses, and see what truth is in God's Word.

1 Thess. 4:13-16

13. But I would not have you to be <u>ignorant,</u> breathren, <u>concerning them which are asleep,</u> that ye sorrow not, even as others <u>which have no hope.</u>

14. For if we believe that Jesus died and <u>rose again,</u> even so <u>them also which sleep in Jesus will God bring with him.</u>

15. For this we say unto you by the word of the Lord, that we which are <u>alive and remain unto the coming of the Lord shall not prevent them which are asleep.</u>

16. For the <u>Lord himself shall descend from heaven</u> with a shout, with the voice of the archangel, and with the trump of God: and the <u>dead in Christ shall rise first:</u> (KJV)

Paul explains in verse 13 and 14 that if you believe that Christ, after his death, rose from the grave, then death is the same to believers. In reality this only means that those who died in Christ will come back with him when he returns to rule and reign, setting up the Millennium. Now in verse 15 we have the word *prevent,* which, when you understand its meaning in the Greek, says a lot about this verse.

5348 phthano (fthan'-o);
apparently a primary verb, to <u>beforehand,
i.e., anticipate or precede; by extension, to
have arrived at:</u>

This word is misleading to the reader of Scripture, in that it can lead you to think that the dead are still in the grave, but in reality they have already been raised, and are with Christ. Therefore those who are with Christ, he will bring with him on his return. To document this we will go to the Book of Jude.

Jude 1:14

14. And Enoch also, the seventh from Adam, prophesied of these, saying, Behold, <u>the Lord cometh with ten thousands of his saints</u>. (KJV)

Verse 16 again in English gives the impression that the dead have not risen yet, but will be raised at the Second Coming of Christ. This is a misunderstanding of Scripture. The word *rise* in the Greek means to "stand up." This is an analogy that these saints will stand up with Christ and come with him, when he comes to set up his kingdom here on earth. They cannot rise up from the grave at the coming of Christ, as this would make Scripture incorrect to what Paul said in 2 Corinthians.

2 Cor. 5:8

8. We are confident, I say, and willing rather to be <u>absent from the body, and to be present with the Lord</u>. (KJV)

Also in Ecclesiastes, it states the following.

Eccles. 12:7

7.   <u>Then shall the dust return to the earth as it was: and the spirit shall return unto God who gave it</u>. (KJV)

Verse 17 is where the Kenites have altered the meanings of these verses, to perpetuate the Rapture theory, and make believers think that they will not have to go through the Great Tribulation. This is one of the great lies of Satan, and the Body of Christ has unwittingly fallen into this trap. If Satan can get you to believe this lie, then when he comes, a lot of believers will believe that Satan is Christ. Let's analyze verse 17.

1 Thess. 4:17

17.   Then we which are <u>alive</u> and <u>remain shall be caught up</u> together <u>with them</u> in the clouds, to meet the Lord in the air; and so shall we ever be with the Lord. (KJV)

When the Scripture refers to those who <u>remain,</u> the Greek meaning is very important. <u>Remain</u> has the following meaning:

4035 perileipo (per-ee-li'po);
from 4012 and 3007; <u>to leave all around,</u> i.e., (passively) <u>survive:</u>

When we look at this meaning, we find that these are the ones who survive the Great Tribulation. They are all around this earth. Paul had to use this word ***remain,*** because he went to the last days concerning Christ's coming. To prove this he stresses that Christ will "descend from heaven with a shout, with the voice of the archangel," as stated in verse 16. He transcended time to show that there will be Saints who survive during the Great Tribulation. When the church did not understand this point, and started to believe in the any- moment theory, Paul then had to write 2 Thessalonians, to clarify that a lot of Scripture had to be fulfilled before Christ would come in his glory.

First and foremost that Satan would have to come first, before Christ could come, and that there would be survivors of the saints, during the Great Tribulation. This only means that the saints who survive, could only be the ones who are living here on earth at Christ's return. More on 2 Thessalonians in this chapter.

Now going further into proof that these are the believers who survive the Great Tribulation, we find that the phrase "with them," is before the words, **"shall be caught up."** This has significant meaning as the word within the Greek means the following.

4862 sun (soon);
a primary preposition denoting union; with or together (but much closer than 3326 or 3844), i.e., by association, companionship, process, resemblance, possession, instrumentality, addition, etc.:

Thus when we look at this meaning, we will be in the same spiritual bodies. We will possess the same type of bodies when we are changed. Going deeper into the meanings of the words underlined, we find that **"shall be caught up"** has one meaning.

726 harpazo (har-pad'-zo);
from a derivative of 138; to seize (in various applications):

The prime root of this word gets us a little closer to its meaning.

138 haireomai (hahee-reh'-om-ahee);
probably akin to 142; to take for oneself, i.e., to prefer:

To put this more plainly, when we take on our spiritual body, it will be like a seizure or a quick happening. The word "cloud" is appropriate, as it is written that he will come in the cloud with great glory. Meeting him in the clouds, when he comes in, is nothing more than meeting him when he returns. The word meet simply means a friendly encounter, of which we and all believers are in anticipation, when we see Jesus. The word "the" was added by the translators and does not belong in this verse. Now the word air is what has confused Christians for a long time. This is what makes people think that they will be raptured from this earth. The Greek meaning makes this furthest from the truth.

109 aer (ah-ayr)');
from semi (to breathe unconsciously, i.e., respire; by analogy, to blow); "air" (as naturally circumambient):
KJV—air. Compare 5594.
***. atha. See 3134.

We will now compare the meanings listed at the bottom of this meaning and see if we can shed more light on this subject.

5594 psucho (psoo'-kho);
a primary verb; to breathe (voluntarily but gently, thus differing on the one hand from 4154, which denotes properly a forcible respiration; and on the other from the base of 109, which refers properly to an inanimate breeze), i.e., (by implication of reduction of temperature by evaporation) to chill (figuratively):

Using all of these meanings, which are underlined for clarity, we find it is the breath, or our breathing that is affected here. This word *air* does not literally mean sky, or does it say that we will be transported up into the sky, to meet those who are coming with Christ at his second coming. The last meaning of 3134 of Aramaic meaning is interesting, that it is tied in with the word *air*.

3134 maran atha (mar'-an ath'-ah);
of Aramaic origin (meaning our Lord has come); maranatha, i.e., an exclamation of the approaching divine judgment:

To show that the word *air* has been misunderstood as "sky" here is the correct Greek meaning for that type of air.

3772 ouranos (oo-ran-os');
perhaps from the same as 3735 (through the idea of elevation); the sky; by extension, heaven (as the abode of God); by implication, happiness, power, eternity; specifically, the Gospel (Christianity):

This word also is used for heaven as well as air in Scripture. Examples are Matt. 8:20 and 13:32.

It says that the Lord is coming, not a rapture. The best way to put this is that we will be changed into spiritual bodies, which will not need the normal breathing, that we have used in this flesh body. So then we should read that verse in this manner.

Then we which are still alive and have survived until the coming of the Lord, will be changed at that moment with those who have passed on before, and come with Christ in the clouds, and we will be transformed from our physical flesh bodies to our spiritual bodies.

This is not a rapture into the air, but a transformation of our bodies. The last line of this verse reveals its true meaning, when it says, "and so shall we ever be with the Lord," which is during the Millennium. When Christ returns he will set up his kingdom on earth, so we will not leave this planet, but rule and reign right here on this old planet earth. Documentation is the Book of Revelation.

Rev. 20:4-5

4. And I saw thrones, and they sat upon them, and judgment was given unto them: and I saw the souls of them that were beheaded for the witness of Jesus, and for the word of God, and which had not worshipped the beast, neither his image, neither had received his mark upon their foreheads, or in their hands; and they <u>lived and reigned with Christ a thousand years</u>.

5. But the rest of the dead lived not again until the thousand years were finished.

This is the first resurrection. (KJV)

Christ's Teaching about His Second Coming

When does the last trump sound and Christ return in his glory? Let us look at what Jesus himself said about his Second Coming in Matthew chapter 24.

Matt. 24:29-31

29. Immediately <u>after the tribulation</u> of those days shall the sun be darkened, and the moon shall not give her light, and the stars shall fall from heaven, and the powers of the heavens shall be shaken:

30. And then shall appear the sign of the Son of man in heaven: and then shall all the tribes of the earth mourn, and they shall see the Son of man coming in the clouds of heaven with power and great glory.

31. And he shall send his angels with a great sound of a trumpet, and they shall <u>gather together his elect from the four winds, from one end of heaven to the other</u>. (KJV)

In verse 29 it states, "Immediately <u>after</u> the tribulation of those days." His coming is <u>after</u> the tribulation. The word *after* is the Greek preposition *meta* and with the accusative, it means simply <u>after.</u> This could be quite a show in the heavens as the moon will not give her light, etc. In verse 30 he declares that this is the time when his elect, or his body will be gathered together, from all over the earth, which is the four winds. Some have said that the "four winds" mean our going up in a rapture. That would not be the truth. When Christ comes he will set up his Kingdom here on earth, which is not in the heavens.

This coincides with 1 Thessalonians 4:17 when the elect are changed into spiritual bodies. Christ is not coming secretly, as the Rapture alleges, but all shall see him, and the tribes of the earth will mourn (Matt. 24:30). This sounds silly, as we see that the King of Kings and the Lord of Lords is coming to set up his kingdom on earth, and you would think that all the people would be glad of his coming. Well, if you just found out that you had worshipped the false Christ, and had been worshipping Antichrist instead, I guess you would be sad and mourn, for now the truth will be known.

Paul says in Ephesians chapter 3 that now the mysteries can be revealed of Christ, and who he is, and made known unto us who believe and study his word. On the other end of all this is Satan, and the Kenites, who do all their deeds in secret. This is why the truth has been distorted in our teaching today.

Why would God allow this to happen? As stated in 2 Thessalonians 2:11, God will send them a delusion, that they should believe a lie. We feel that the Rapture theory is a part of this lie, which will keep most believers from knowing the truth in the end times, and worshipping Antichrist when he comes.

Second Coming As Told by Jesus

We saw earlier that Jesus said in Matthew 24 that after this Great Tribulation his coming would take place. Is there anything in his foretelling of the end times that suggest that a rapture would take place? We will go into this chapter in Matthew in which our Lord told his disciples, when asked what would happen at the end of this earth age. Starting off in the beginning of this chapter, we read the following.

Matt. 24:1-2

1. And Jesus went out, and departed from the temple: and his disciples came to him for to shew him the buildings of the temple.

2. And Jesus said unto them, See ye not all these things? verily I say unto you. there shall <u>not be left here one stone upon another, that shall not be thrown down</u>. (KJV)

Most scholars believe that this prophecy has already been fulfilled, when the Roman centurion Titus invaded Jerusalem and burned it down. But if we look at the second verse, we see that Jesus said that there would not be <u>one stone left upon another.</u> Did Titus destroy the temple completely? No. There are still parts of this temple left. The Wailing Wall is one example, as it is a part of the original temple from that era.

Archaeologists are still uncovering parts of that temple and finding rooms intact. History records that the temple was sacked and burned, but they did not dismantle the temple stone by stone. What Christ was talking about is a complete annihilation, in which there will be nothing left but complete rubble. This has not happened yet and will not happen, until Christ comes and destroys the temple, recreated by Satan and makes it a heap. We will go into this more as we get further into this chapter. But this makes it an end-time prophecy. Let's continue on in this chapter to further document that this is an end-time event.

Matt. 24:3

3. And as he sat upon the Mount of Olives, the disciples came nto him privately, saying, Tell us, <u>when shall these things be?</u> and what shall <u>be the sign of thy coming, and of the end of the world</u>? (KJV)

As his disciples inquired into when these things be, they understood that the temple was a part of the end times. Looking at the meaning of "end of the world," we find the following meaning for **"world."**

165 aion (ahee-ohn');
from the same as 104; properly, <u>an age;</u> by extension, perpetuity (also past); by implication, the world; especially (Jewish); a <u>Messianic period</u> (present or <u>future</u>):

They asked for a sign of his coming. The word *world* in this context, means the end of this earth age. Concerning future events that would herald his second coming. His disciples were taught by Christ and knew of the different ages, that were before, that were present, and also to come. Now let's get into what Jesus had to say about what will happen in the end times.

Matt. 24:4-8

4. And Jesus answered and said unto them, Take heed that no man deceive you.

5. For many shall come in my name, saying, <u>I am Christ;</u> and shall <u>deceive many.</u>

6. And ye shall hear of <u>wars and rumours of wars;</u> see that ye be not troubled: for <u>all these things must come to pass,</u> but the end <u>is not yet.</u>

7. For <u>nation shall rise against nation, and kingdom against kingdom:</u> and there shall be <u>famines, and pestilences,</u> and <u>earthquakes, in divers places.</u>

8. All these are the <u>beginning of sorrows.</u> (KJV)

Here is where it will all start. There are a lot of theologians who say that that Antichrist is a man empowered by Satan. What we feel will happen, is that a false Antichrist will come onto the scene, who will be a man, and who will be possessed with demonic spirits and have great power.

He will start to set up the one- world system. This will cause a lot of havoc in the world. There will be fighting among the people and the nations, as the pangs of this New World Order are in the process of being put into place, by this false Antichrist. We also believe that after this false Antichrist is on the scene, a lot of Christians will not be deceived, as they know that Antichrist comes first. This first Antichrist we feel is the False Prophet. Then Satan will come as the real Antichrist, and this will be the great deception.

2 Thessalonians

A lot of emphasis has been put on the second chapter of 2 Thessalonians as proof of the Rapture, that this will take place. Let's analyze this chapter and see if we can ascertain what the Apostle Paul was talking about.

2 Thess. 2:1-3

1. Now we beseech you, brethren, by the <u>coming of our Lord Jesus Christ, and by our gathering together unto him.</u>

2. That ye be <u>not soon shaken in mind, or be troubled, neither by spirit, nor by word, nor by letter as from us,</u> as that the day of Christ is at hand.

3. <u>Let no man deceive you</u> by any means: for that <u>day shall not come, except there came a falling away first, and that man of sin be revealed, the son of perdition;</u> (KJV)

In these first 3 verses of this chapter, Paul apparently has heard that the church of the Thessalonians was having a problem with the theory that Christ could come any moment, and Paul was trying to set this doctrine straight. In verse 3 he explains why they did not have to be worried about Christ coming at any moment, because that man of sin had to be revealed first. The son of perdition is none other than Satan or Antichrist himself.

This shows the readers that Satan has to come on the scene before Christ can come down in his <u>Second Coming.</u> It seems to be self-evident that Paul is also saying that you will be here at this time. Therefore by this statement, it does not seem like a rapture. Moving on in this chapter, we will gather more evidence of this conclusion.

2 Thess. 2:4-10

4. <u>Who opposeth and exalteth himself above all that is called God,</u> or that <u>is wor-shipped; so that he as God sitteth in the temple of God, shewing himself that he is God.</u>

5. Remember ye not, that, when I was yet with you, I told you these things?

6. And now ye know what <u>withholdeth</u> that he might be revealed in his time.

7. For the <u>mystery of iniquity doth already work: only he who now letteth will let, un-til he be taken out of the way.</u>

8. And <u>then shall that Wicked be revealed, whom the Lord shall consume with the spirit of his mouth, and shall destroy with the brightness of his coming;</u>

9. Even him, whose coming is after the work-ing of Satan with all power and signs and lying wonders,

10. And with all deceivableness of unright-eousness in them that perish; because they received not the love of the truth, that they might be saved. (KJV)

Who is Paul talking about in verse 4? None other than Satan himself. Verse 8 of the above Scriptures is a startling disclosure, that in the manuscript after Lord, the actual name of Jesus was used. It should read, "whom the Lord Jesus shall consume, etc." What we feel happened here was that the Kenites in translation of the King James version omitted the name Jesus after Lord. And therefore the tradition of the omission of Jesus' name is still carried on today, which perpetuates the theory of a rapture making one believe that the Holy Spirit and believers are gone, while in reality this is talking about Jesus' actual physical return to earth, which will start the Millenium or his thousand year reign. Jesus' real name in Greek is as follows.

2424 Iesous (ee-ay-sooce');
of Hebrew origin [3091]; <u>Jesus (i.e., Jehoshua), the name of our Lord</u> and two (three) other Israelites:
KJV—Jesus.

The Kenites were successful in omitting the actual name of Jesus to give the reader the illusion that the absence of the Holy Spirit is how Satan will be revealed, voiding Christ's actual physical return. The word **"destroy"** has the following meaning:

2673 katargeo (kat-arg-eh'-o);
from 2596 and 691; <u>to be (render) entirely idle (useless), literally or figuratively:</u>

This shows that Satan will not be physically destroyed, but as written in Revelation 20:2, is locked in chains until the end of the Millennium.

Satan opposes God and will in the end times sit in the temple as God, as Christ referred to in Matthew.

Matt. 24:15

15. When ye therefore shall <u>see the abomina-
    tion of desolation, spoken of by Daniel
    the prophet, stand in the holy place, (who-
    so readeth, let him understand:</u>) (KJV)

It was also spoken of in the Book of Mark.

Mark 13:14

14. But when <u>ye shall set the abomination of
    desolation, spoken of by Daniel the
    prophet, standing where it ought not,</u> (let
    him that readeth understand,) then let
    them that be in Judaea flee to the moun-
    tains: (KJV)

What is interesting about these verses is that
Jesus said, "<u>ye</u> shall <u>see</u> the abomination of
desolation." If we can see the abomination of Satan sitting where he ought not, then we would
still have to be here on earth, as Satan will be
cast out of heaven by Michael the archangel,
down to this earth as spoken of in Revelation
12:7-9. In Daniel he also speaks of Michael
standing up on behalf of his people and that Michael is referred to as a prince.

Dan. 12:1

1. And at that that shall Michael stand up,
   <u>the great prince</u> which standeth for the
   children of thy people: <u>and there shall be a
   time of trouble, such as never was since
   there was a nation even to that same time:</u>
   and at that time thy people shall be delivered, every one that shall be found written
   in the book. (KJV)

It is noted that this verse depicts a time of

great turmoil that was never seen before and will never be again. This coincides with what Jesus referred to in Matthew 24:21- 23 about the Great Tribulation, and also warning us about a false Christ, which will come first. Another mistranslation of Scripture is in Matthew 24:24. When this verse speaks of false Christs, this is in reality only one, which is Satan himself. The term **"false Christ"** is one that has the following meaning:

5580 pseudochristos (psyoo-dokh'-ris-tos);
from 5571 and 5547; a spurious Messiah:

The capitalizing of Christ only shows that this is one entity, along with the meaning of this word showing the spurious Messiah who is Satan himself. There even Jesus himself states that Satan will be here before him.

Going back to verse 6 of 2 Thessalonians, it states "now you know what withholdeth." This word has an explicit meaning.

2722 katecho (kat-ekh'-o);
from 2596 and 2192; to hold down (fast), in various applications (literally or figuratively):

Satan is held down fast in heaven until his time to be revealed. Daniel the prophet speaks of Michael holding back Satan. This will only happen when it is God's time to set all this in motion. Going into verse 7, we will find a highly controversial verse. Many ministers refer to this as the Rapture verse, and that it proves that the Rapture will take place.

The idea behind this reasoning is that a lot of ministers claim that this is when the Holy Spirit is taken out of the way, to make room for Antichrist to work, and that "he who now letteth is the Holy Spirit." This theory would be very inconsistent with God's Word.

We know that it is the Spirit that draws men unto Christ. Then during the Great Tribulation, a lot of souls will lose their lives for Christ's name sake. If the Holy Spirit is gone, then what convicts them to stand fast for Jesus' name? To document this we will go to Revelation.

Rev. 6:9-11

9.   And when he had opened the fifth seal, I saw under the altar the <u>souls of them that were slain for the word of God, and for</u> the <u>testimony which they held:</u>

10. And they cried with a loud voice, saying, <u>How long, O Lord,</u> holy and true, dost thou not judge and <u>avenge our blood on them that dwell on the earth?</u>

11. And white robes were given unto every one of them; and it was said unto them, that they should <u>rest yet for a little season, until their fellow servants also and their brethren, that should be killed as they were, should be fulfilled</u>. (KJV)

This is proof that some will be killed during the Great Tribulation, as these verses are talking about end-time prophecy. It is noted that those who go first, will have to wait a little season until the others are slain because of their belief in Christ, meaning that the Holy Spirit will still be here to convict, and to guide those who are here during this time of troubles. It is also written that Jesus said "I will never leave you nor forsake you."

Going further into this verse, we find that the word *letteth* is the same word that was used in the previous verse, meaning to hold fast. The words **will let** were added by the translators and are not in the original manuscripts. What this verse really says is that Satan is being held down fast until he is kicked out of heaven by Michael. This word is a verb, which shows who the subject is, and it is Satan. Verse 9 states that Christ will not come until <u>after</u> the working of Satan on this earth. This could not be any plainer. Christ cannot appear until after the working of Satan.

This chapter goes on to say just what we have been trying to say, only better.

2 Thess. 2:11-12

11. And for <u>this cause God shall send them strong delusion, that they should believe a lie:</u>

12. That they <u>all might be damned who believed not the truth,</u> but had pleasure in unrighteousness. (KJV)

So then the Rapture is a lie, and those who believe in it could be damned if they do not recognize the truths, so eloquently written in God's Word.

The One Taken and the Other Left

Many a preacher has taught that the verses below concerning those working when one is taken and the other left, describe the Rapture. If you go into the meanings of these verses, you will find a different meaning.

Matt. 24:40 11

40. Then shall <u>two be in the field;</u> the one shall be <u>taken,</u> and the other left.

41. Two women shall be grinding at the mill; the one shall be <u>taken,</u> and the other <u>left.</u>

42. <u>Watch</u> therefore: for <u>ye know not what hour your Lord doth come.</u>

43. But know this, that if the goodman of the house <u>had known in what watch the thief would come, he would have watched, and would not have suffered his house to be broken up.</u>

44. Therefore <u>be ye also ready:</u> for in such an hour as ye think not the Son of man cometh. (KJV)

The analogy of verse 40, in which two shall be in the field, brings to mind the parable of the tares. In this parable, Christ talks about a field where the good seed is sown. Then they find out that Satan has sown bad seed, also into this field. We feel that this is pertinent in this verse. Now the words *taken* and *left* when looked at in the Greek have the following meanings:

3880 paralambano (par-al-am-ban'-o);
from 3844 and 2983; <u>to receive near,</u> i.e., <u>associate with oneself (in any familiar or intimate act or relation);</u> by analogy, to assume an office; <u>figuratively, of learn:</u>

If we go into *Thayer's* definition of *taken,* we can get a clearer picture of this word.

3880 paralambano-

1. to take to, to take with oneself, <u>to join to oneself</u>
   a) <u>an associate,</u> a companion
   b) metaphorically:
1. <u>to accept or acknowledge one to be such as he professes to be</u>
2. <u>not to reject,</u> not to withhold obedience
3. to receive something transmitted
   a) an office to be discharged
   b) <u>to receive with the mind</u>

This makes it abundantly clear that the person is not actually taken, but joins themselves unto the current system. They will associate themselves with Antichrist, and be taught the lie, that Satan is the Messiah. Now let's look at the word **"left"** and see just what we can derive from its Greek meaning.

863 aphiemi (af-ee'-ay-mee);

from 575 and hiemi <u>(to send;</u> an intensive form of eimi, to go); <u>to send forth,</u> in various applications

We will break this down in *Thayer's* definition, which can also clarify this word a little better.

863 aphiemi-

1. to send away
   a) to bid going away or <u>to depart:</u> used of a <u>husband divorcing his wife</u>
   b) to send forth, to yield up, to expire
   c) to let go, to let alone, to let be
      1. <u>to disregard</u>
      2. to leave, not to discuss now, (a topic);

3. used of teachers, writers and speakers

4. to omit, to neglect

d) <u>to let go,</u> to give up a debt, to forgive, to remit

e) to give up, <u>to keep no longer</u>

2. to permit, to allow, not to hinder, <u>to give up a thing to a person</u>

Verses 42-45 just prove what Christ was talking about, his Second Coming. If we are to watch to keep the thief from stealing our house, then Christ has not appeared as yet.

As we look at these definitions, we get a clear picture that these are not left here on earth, but as spoken of in Revelation, that they come out of Babylon. It is clear that the people that Christ referred to in these verses, left the false bridegroom, and came out of confusion. The ones that the King James Version says were taken, are in reality, taken unto Antichrist himself. Therefore these could not be Rapture verses. They deal with those going and associating themselves with the false messiah, and those who come out of this confusion, and hear and understand the truth, that Christ has not come yet, are waiting for his return. A lot of them will be killed as stated previously when we quoted Revelation chapter 6.

The Ten Virgins

Many believe that the parable of the ten virgins is an example of the Rapture taking place. Showing in the previous part of this chapter that some will go and wed themselves with Antichrist and some will hold onto the testimony of Jesus, we will go into this account in Matthew, concerning the ten virgins, to correlate between this account of the people who were taken, and those who were left.

Matt. 25:1-2

1. Then shall the kingdom of heaven be likened unto <u>ten virgins, which took their lamps, and went forth to meet the bridgeroom,</u> 20 And <u>five of them were wise, and five were foolish</u>. (KJV)

In this verse it says that went out to meet the bridegroom. What bridegroom did they go out to meet? Because later on we will read of another bridegroom coming. This we feel is the false bridegroom, which comes first. In verse 2 it was written in the manuscripts that the five foolish were identified before the five wise. The foolish no doubt believed that they had found the right bridegroom. Let's go further into this chapter to see the five wise had what the foolish did not.

Matt. 25:3-5

3. They that were foolish <u>took their lamps, and took no oil with them:</u>

4. But the wise <u>took oil in their vessels</u> with their lamps.

5. While the <u>bridegroom tarried,</u> they all slumbered and slept. (KJV)

The oil spoken of here is a figure of speech for knowledge or teaching of the truth. This is the same oil poured into the bow and candlestick, the two witnesses, spoken of in the last chapter. They use this oil or truth, to witness to the people in these last days. Without the truth your lamps cannot burn brightly, when the Lord comes to claim his own. Verse 5 states that the bridegroom tarried. This shows that Christ had not come, for he is the true bridegroom whom we are waiting for. Now what happened when the true bridegroom comes, is recorded the next verses.

Matt. 25:6-12

6.   And <u>at midnight</u> there was a cry made. <u>Behold the bridegroom</u> cometh;<u> go ye out to meet him.</u>

7.   Then all those virgins <u>arose, and trimmed their lamps.</u>

8.   And the <u>foolish</u> said unto the wise, <u>give us of your oil; for our lamps are gone out.</u>

9.   But the wise answered, saying, <u>Not so; lest there be not enough for us and you: but go ye rather to them that sell, and buy for yourselves.</u>

10.   And while they went to buy, <u>the bridegroom came;</u> and <u>they that were ready went in with him to the marriage; and the door was shut.</u>

11.   Afterward came also the other virgins, saying, Lord, Lord, open to us.

12.   But he answered and said, Verily I say unto you, <u>I know you not</u>. (KJV)

The word **"foolish"** has a particularly appropriate meaning.

3474 moros (mo-ros');
probably from the base of 3466; <u>dull or stupid</u> (as if shut up), i.e., heedless, (morally) <u>block-head, (apparently) absurd:</u>

This, simply put, shows how traditions being used in the churches of today, hinders the real truth. Some Christians cannot change their views, because they are so stuck on their traditions. An example of this, in our experience, when dealing with Christians faced by this knowledge, they would use the comment "I don't care what you say, they will not be here." This is the blockheaded attitude that Christ was alluding to.

Now we will look at the word *trim* and see just what is its meaning.

2885 kosmeo (kos-meh'-o);
from 2889; <u>to put in proper order,</u> i.e., decorate (literally or figuratively); especially, to snuff (a wick):

Looking at the word *wise,* we also find out why these virgins listened, and did as they were told.

5429 phronimos (fro n' -ee-mos);
from 5424; <u>thoughtful, i.e., sagacious or discreet</u> (implying a cautious character, while 4680 denotes practical skill or acumen; and 4908 indicates rather <u>intelligence or mental acquirement);</u> in a bad sense conceited (also in the comparative):

Here the wise used the teachings of wisdom,

taught them by the two olive trees to understand that the false Messiah was here on earth. This is spoken of in Revelation.

Then the wise put things in order, and knew that Antichrist had to come before Christ the real Messiah would come. They also knew that they would not be raptured out, but would be here during the Great Tribulation.

Rev. 7:1-4

1. And after these things I saw four angels standing on the four corners of the earth, holding the four winds of the earth, that the wind should not blow on the earth, nor on the sea, nor on any tree.

2. And I saw another angel ascending from the east, having the seal of the living God and he cried with a loud voice to the four angels, to whom it was given to hurt the earth and the sea.

3. Saying, <u>Hurt not the earth, neither the sea, nor the trees, till we have sealed the servants of our God in their foreheads.</u>

4. And I heard the number of them which were sealed, and there were sealed a hundred and forty and four thousand of all the tribes of the children of Israel. (KJV)

Although these verses refer to the 144,000 of the tribes of Israel, it does not include those others who came out of the Great Tribulation also which were sealed.

9. After this I beheld, and, lo, <u>a great multitude, which no man could number,</u> of <u>all nations, and kindreds, and people, and tongues,</u> stood before the throne, and before the Lamb, clothed with <u>white robes,</u> and palms in their hands;

10. And cried with a loud voice, saying, Salvation to our God which sitteth upon the throne, and unto the Lamb.

11. And all the angels stood round about the throne, and about the elders and the four beasts, and fell before the throne on their faces, and worshipped God,

12. Saying, Amen, Blessing, and glory, and wisdom, and thanksgiving, and honour, and power, and might, be unto our God for ever and ever. Amen.

13. And one of the elders answered, saying unto me, What are hese which are arrayed in white robes? And whence came they?

14. And I said unto him, Sir, thou knowest. And he said to me, These are they which <u>came out of great tribulation,</u> and have <u>washed their robes,</u> and made them white in the blood of the Lamb. (KJV)

Here is the meat of this matter. When the true Messiah came, five were not ready. Their lights were out. They had believed that the first bridegroom was the Messiah, and did not accept the truth. Therefore there lamps were not oiled and trimmed.

The five wise who knew the truth,, and kept their lights ready, to meet with our Lord at his coming. When the others asked for some oil from the wise, they told them to go and buy theirs. In other words they must pay the price, by testifying or with martyrdom.

This reminds us of Revelation, which speaks of the mark of the beast and, only through him can you buy and sell. It then goes on to say that when Christ came he closed the door. When the foolish came back and asked to come in, Christ told them that he never knew them. What a shock this will be to some who think they have the truth.

Heaven and Earth Passing Away

Many teachers of God's Word have used the following Scriptures, to not only perpetuate the Rapture Theory, but to give credence to, "he will come at any moment" theory.

Matt. 24:34-36

34. Verily I say unto you, <u>this generation shall not pass,</u> till all <u>these things be fulfilled.</u>

35. <u>Heaven and earth shall pass away, but my words shall not pass away.</u>

36. But of that <u>day and hour knoweth no man,</u> no, <u>not the angels of heaven, but my Father only.</u> (KJV)

Many have used the word *generation* as a certain period of years. Example: some say 40 years while others use 90 or 120 to denote a generation. Just what does this word mean?

1074 genea (ghehn-eh-ah');
from (a presumed derivative of) 1085; a generation; by implication, <u>an age</u> (the period or the persons):

This is very revealing in that Christ was not talking about a few years, but this <u>earth age.</u> The fact that <u>all things</u> must be fulfilled, simply means that every event that has been prophesied, has to be fulfilled. This includes the releasing of Satan after the Millennium, and also the judgment, which will take place after Satan is defeated. This has been overlooked by most scholars, that <u>all things</u> have to be fulfilled. For further documentation, we will look at some other highly misunderstood verses in 1 Corinthians.

1 Cor. 15:49-56

49. And as we have borne the <u>image of the earthly,</u> we shall also bear the <u>image of the heavenly.</u>

50. Now this I say, brethren, that <u>flesh and blood cannot inherit the kingdom of God; neither doth corruption inherit incorruption.</u>

51. Behold, I shew you a mystery; We shall not <u>all sleep,</u> but we shall <u>all be changed.</u>

52. In a moment, in the twinkling of an eye, at the last trump for the trumpet shall sound, and the dead shall be raised incorruptible, and we shall be changed.

53. For this corruptible shall have put on in-corporation, and this mortal shall have put on immortality.

54. So when this corruptible shall have put on incorruption, and this mortal shall have put on immortality, then shall be brought to pass the saying that is written, <u>Death is swallowed up in victory.</u>

55. <u>0 death, where is thy sting? 0 grave, where is thy victory?</u>

56. The sting of death is sin; and the strength of sin is the law. (KJV)

Many believe that this also includes the Rapture. This is not truth. We <u>read not all will sleep, but all will be changed.</u> The key to these verses is in verse 54, where death is swallowed up in victory. Who is death? Satan himself and his deception, will be death to those who follow him. So in victory, when Satan and his followers are destroyed, then there will be no death. When the New Heaven and New Earth comes down, all death will be wiped away, and the grave will be gone. No death will ever happen again, when we rule and reign with God in eternity. Further documentation of this truth is found in 1 Corinthians again:

1 Cor. 15:22-28

22. For as in Adam all die, even so in Christ shall all be made alive.

23. But every man in his own order: <u>Christ the firstfruits;</u> afterward they that are Christ's at his coming.

24. <u>Then cometh the end,</u> when he shall have delivered up the kingdom to God, even the Father; when he shall have put down all rule and all authority and power.

25. For he must reign, till he hath put all enemies under his feet.

26. <u>The last enemy that shall be destroyed is death.</u>

27. For he hath put all things under his feet. But when he saith, all things are put under him; it is manifest that he is excepted, which did put all things under him.

28. And when all things shall be subdued unto him, then shall the Son also himself be subject unto him that put all things under him, that <u>God may be all in all</u>. (KJV)

To show that all falls in line in fulfillment with Scripture, we will go to Revelation.

Rev. 20:1-5

1. And I saw an angel come down from heaven, having the key of the bottomless pit and a great chain in his hand.

2. And he laid hold on the dragon, that old serpent, which is the Devil, and Satan, and bound him a <u>thousand years.</u>

3. And cast him into the bottomless pit, and shut him up, and set a seal upon him, that he should deceive the nations no more, till <u>the thousand years should be fulfilled:</u> and after that he must be <u>loosed a little season.</u>

4. And I saw thrones, and they sat upon them, <u>and judgment</u> was given unto them: and I saw the <u>souls of them that were beheaded for the witness of Jesus,</u> and for the word of God, and which had <u>not worshipped the beast, neither his image, neither had received his mark upon their foreheads, or in their hands;</u> and they lived and reigned with Christ a thousand years.

5. But the rest of the dead lived not again until the thousand years were finished. <u>This is the first resurrection</u>. (KJV)

What we have here is the beginning of the Millennium, and putting Satan under control through incarceration. Those who went through the Great Tribulation and did not receive his mark, would live and reign with Christ for a thousand years. This will also bring to fulfillment that which was spoken by Isaiah the prophet.

Isa. 14:16.

16. They that see thee shall narrowly look upon thee, and consider thee, saying, <u>Is this the man</u> that made the earth to tremble, that did shake kingdoms; (KJV)

So therefore, those who did not receive the mark, will be transformed into spiritual bodies, which is the first resurrection of the firstfruits. Many think that the first resurrection was only when Christ arose from the grave. This is true except that when Christ arose he also made it possible for all who died after, would also be resurrected. Paul said it plainly.

1 Cor. 15:12-14

12. Now if Christ be preached that <u>he rose from the dead,</u> how say some among you that there is no resurrection of the dead?

13. But if there be <u>no resurrection of the dead, then is Christ not risen;</u>

14. And if <u>Christ be not risen, then is our preaching vain,</u> and your faith is also vain. (KJV)

To document this point a little further, we will go into Revelation.

Rev. 20:6-9

6. Blessed and holy is he that hath part in the first resurrectionon such the second death hath no power, but they shall be priests of God and of Christ, and shall reign with him a thousand years.

7. <u>And when the thousand years are expired, Satan shall be loosed</u> out of <u>his prison.</u>

8. And shall go out to deceive the nations which are in the four quarters of the earth, <u>Gog and Magog,</u> to gather them together to battle the number of whom is as the sand of the sea.

9. And they went up on the breadth of the earth, and compassed the camp of the saints about, and the beloved city: <u>and fire came down</u> from God out of heaven, and devoured them.

It is noteworthy here that this event takes place after the thousand years, and Satan according to

Verse 8 goes back to Gog and Magog, which is spoken of in Ezekiel 38. Many have said that Ezekiel's chapter 38 deals with the Great Tribulation, but this shows conclusively that it is after. In reference to verse 9, this is a fulfillment of Ezekiel's prophecy.

Ezek. 28:18-19.

18. Thou hast defiled thy sanctuaries by the multitude of thine iniquities, by the iniquity of thy traffick; <u>therefore will I bring forth a fire from the midst of thee, it shall devour thee,</u> and I will bring thee to ashes upon the earth in the sight of all them that behold thee.

19. And they that know thee among the people shall be astonished at thee: thou shalt be a terror, and never shalt thou be any more. (KJV)

The rest of this chapter is justification that all has to be fulfilled before death is swallowed up in victory.

Rev. 20:10-15

10. And the <u>devil that deceived them was cast into the lake of fire</u> and brimstone, where the beast and the false prophet are, and shall be tormented day and night for ever and ever.

11. And J saw a great white throne, and him that sat on it, from whose face the earth and the heaven fled away; and there was found no place for them.

12. And I saw the dead, small and great, stand

before God; and the books were opened: and another book was opened, which is the book of life: and the dead were judged out of those things which were written in the books, according to their works.

13. And the sea gave up the dead which were in it; and death and hell delivered up the dead which were in them: and they were judged every man according to their works_

14. And death and hell were cast into the lake of fire. <u>This is the second death.</u>

15. And whosoever was <u>not found written in the book of life was cast into the lake of fire</u>. (KJV)

Rev. 21:1

1. And I saw a <u>new heaven and a new earth:</u> for the first heaven and the first earth were passed away; and there was no more sea.

We can almost imagine the horror when Christ appears on earth, that the following Scriptures take place and those who have taught this lie, have to listen to these words from Jesus.

Matt. 7:22-23

22. <u>Many will say to me in that day, Lord, Lord, have we not prophesied in thy name? And in thy name have cast out devils? And in thy name done many wonderful works?</u>

23. And then will I <u>profess unto them, I never knew you: depart from me, yet that work iniquity</u>. (KJV)

The authors hope that what we have revealed in this book will help our Christian brothers and sisters to look more closely into the Word of God. If some of you, who have read this book, have not made a commitment to Christ, we invite you to use the following verse, and really confess that Christ is Lord of your life.

Rom. 10:9

9. That if thou shalt <u>confess with thy mouth the Lord Jesus,</u> and shalt <u>believe in thine heart that God hath raised him from the dead, thou shalt be saved</u>. (KJV)

If you have followed this simple message, then you are in the body of Christ. You do not need to call someone on the phone to confess, but confess in the privacy of your own home, or wherever you may be, and receive our Lord and Saviour Jesus Christ into your hearts. God bless all you have read and understood what we have put forth in this book, and may the love of God bless and keep you unto the end.